WHAT IS IT LIKE TO DIE?

"All pain vanished."

"I went through this dark, black vacuum at super speed."

"There was a feeling of utter peace and quiet, no fear at all."

"I was in a very dark, very deep valley. Later I thought, 'Well, now I know what the Bible means by *the valley of the shadow of death* because I've been there.'"

"After I came back, I cried off and on for about a week because I had to live in this world after seeing that one."

"It opened up a whole new world for me . . . I kept thinking, 'There's so much that I've got to find out.'"

"I heard a voice telling me what I had to do—go back—and I felt no fear."

LIFE AFTER LIFE

The investigation of a phenomenon—
survival of bodily death

RAYMOND A. MOODY, JR.

With a foreword by
Elisabeth Kubler-Ross, M.D.

LIFE AFTER LIFE

*A Bantam Book / published by arrangement with
Mockingbird Books*

PRINTING HISTORY

Mockingbird edition published November 1975
2nd printing .. December 1975
3rd printing ..... March 1976
4th printing ...... May 1976
Bantam edition / November 1976

2nd printing .. November 1976	*6th printing .. December 1976*
3rd printing .. November 1976	*7th printing .... January 1977*
4th printing .. November 1976	*8th printing ... February 1977*
5th printing .. December 1976	*9th printing ... February 1977*

10th printing
11th printing
12th printing
13th printing
14th printing
15th printing
16th printing

Bantam Books are published by Bantam Books, Inc. Its trademark, consisting of the words "Bantam Books" and the portrayal of a bantam, is registered in the United States Patent Office and in other countries. Marca Registrada. Bantam Books, Inc., 666 Fifth Avenue, New York, New York 10019.

PRINTED IN THE UNITED STATES OF AMERICA

*To George Ritchie, M.D.
and, through him, to the
One whom he suggested.*

Acknowledgments

There have been very many people who have given me assistance and encouragement during my research and writing, and I could not have completed this project without them. It was my good friend John Ouzts who talked me into giving my first public talk on this subject. John Egle of Mockingbird Books first encouraged me to commit my findings to writing, and has provided support and encouragement throughout. Leonard, Mae, Becky, and Scott Brooks provided room, board, and taxi service for me on many occasions when I needed them. Kathy Tabakian accompanied me on several interviews, and I benefited from long discussions of them with her. Russ Moores, Richard Martin, and Ed McCranie, all of the Medical College of Georgia, offered valuable suggestions and referred me to much relevant literature. My wife spent long hours editing the manuscript and typescript. Finally, I should like most of all to thank all those who told me of their encounters with death. I can only hope that this book is worthy of all the confidence that everyone mentioned above has placed in me.

CONTENTS

FOREWORD

I have had the privilege of reading the pre-publication copy of Dr. Moody's *Life After Life*, and I am delighted that this young scholar has the courage to put his findings together and make this new type of research available to the general public.

Since I have worked with terminally ill patients over the last two decades, I have become more and more preoccupied with looking into the phenomena of death itself. We have learned a lot about the process of dying, but we still have many questions with regard to the moment of death and to the experience our patients have when they are pronounced medically dead.

It is research such as Dr. Moody presents in his book that will enlighten many and will confirm what we have been taught for two thousand years—that there is life after death. Though he does not claim to have studied death itself, it is evident from his findings that the dying patient continues to have a conscious awareness of his environment after being pronounced clinically dead. This very much coincides with my own research, which has used the accounts of patients who have died and made a comeback, totally against our expectations and often to the surprise of some highly sophisticated, well-known and certainly accomplished physicians.

All of these patients have experienced a floating out of their physical bodies, associated with a great sense of peace and wholeness. Most were aware of another person who helped them in their transition to another plane of existence. Most were greeted by loved ones who had died before them, or by a religious figure who was significant in their life and who coincided, naturally, with their own religious beliefs. It is enlightening to read Dr. Moody's book at the time when I am ready to put my own research findings on paper.

Dr. Moody will have to be prepared for a lot of criticism, mainly from two areas. There will be members of the clergy who will be upset by anyone who dares to do research in an area which is supposed to be taboo. Some religious representatives of a denominational church have already expressed their criticism of studies like this. One priest referred to it as "selling cheap grace." Others simply felt that the question of life after death should remain an issue of blind faith and should not be questioned by anyone. The second group of people that Dr. Moody can expect to respond to his book with concern are scientists and physicians who regard this kind of study as "unscientific."

I think we have reached an era of transition in our society. We have to have the courage to open new doors and admit that our present-day scientific tools are inadequate for many of these new investigations. I think that this book will open these new doors for people who can have an open mind, and it will give them hope and courage to evaluate new areas of research. They will know that this account of Dr. Moody's findings is true, because it is written by a genuine and honest investigator. It is also corroborated by my own research and by the findings of other very serious-minded scientists, scholars and members of the clergy who have had the courage to investigate in this new field of research in the hope of helping those who need to know, rather than to believe.

I recommend this book to anyone with an open mind, and I congratulate Dr. Moody for the courage to put his findings into print.

ELISABETH KUBLER–ROSS, M.D.

Flossmoor, Illinois

LIFE
AFTER
LIFE

INTRODUCTION

This book, written as it is by a human being, naturally reflects the background, opinions and prejudices of its author. So, although I have tried to be as objective and straightforward as I can, certain facts about me might be useful in evaluating some of the extraordinary claims which are made in what follows.

First of all, I have never been close to death myself, so I am not giving a firsthand account of experiences which I have had myself. At the same time I cannot claim total objectivity on that basis, since my emotions have become involved in this project. In hearing so many people relate the fascinating experiences with which this volume deals, I have come to feel almost as though I have lived through them myself. I can only hope that this attitude has not compromised the rationality and balance of my approach.

Secondly, I write as a person who is not broadly familiar with the vast literature on paranormal and occult phenomena. I do not say this to disparage it, and I feel confident that a wider acquaintance with it might have increased my understanding of the events I have studied. In fact, I intend now to look more closely at some of these writings to see to what extent the investigations of others are borne out by my findings.

Thirdly, my religious upbringing deserves some comment. My family attended the Presbyterian Church, yet my parents never tried to impose their religious beliefs or concepts upon their children. They generally tried, as I was growing up, to encourage whatever interests I developed on my own and provided the opportunity for me to pursue them. So, I have grown up having a "religion" not as a set of fixed doctrines, but rather as a concern with spiritual and religious doctrines, teachings, and questions. I believe that all the great religions of man have many truths to tell us, and I believe that no one of us has all the answers to the deep and fundamental truths with which religion deals. In organizational terms, I am a member of the Methodist Church.

Fourthly, my academic and professional background is somewhat diverse—some would say fractured. I attended graduate school in philosophy at the University of Virginia and received my Ph.D. in that subject in 1969. My areas of special interest in philosophy are ethics, logic, and the philosophy of language. After teaching philosophy for three years at a university in eastern North Carolina, I decided to go to medical school, and I intend to become a psychiatrist and to teach the philosophy of medicine in a medical school. All these interests and experiences necessarily helped shape the approach I have taken in this study.

My hope for this book is that it will draw attention to a phenomenon which is at once very widespread and very well-hidden, and, at the same time, help create a more receptive public attitude toward it. For it is my firm conviction that this phenomenon has great significance, not only for many academic and practical fields—especially psychology, psychiatry, medicine, philosophy, theology, and the ministry—but also for the way in which we lead our daily lives.

Let me say at the very beginning that, on grounds which I will explain much later, I am not trying to prove that there is life after death. Nor do I think that a "proof" of this is presently possible. Partly for this reason, I have avoided the use of actual names and have disguised certain identifying details in the stories, while leaving their contents unchanged. This has been necessary, both to protect the privacy of the individuals concerned and, in many cases, to be granted permission to publish the experience related to me in the first place.

There will be many who will find the claims made in this book incredible and whose first reaction will be to dismiss them out of hand. I have no room whatsoever to blame anyone who finds himself in this category; I would have had precisely the same reaction only a few years ago. I am not asking that anyone accept and believe the contents of this volume on my authority alone. Indeed, as a logician who disavows that road to belief which proceeds through invalid appeals to authority, I specifically ask that no one do so. All I ask is for anyone who disbelieves what he reads here to poke around a bit for himself. I have issued this challenge repeatedly for some time. Of those who have accepted it, there have been very many who, skeptical at first, have come to share my bafflement over these events.

On the other hand, there no doubt will be many who read this and find in it a great relief, for they will discover that they are not alone in having had such an experience. To them—especially if, like most, they have concealed their story from all but a few trusted persons—I can only say this: It is my hope that this volume may encourage you to speak a little more freely, so that a most intriguing facet of the human soul may be more clearly elucidated.

1
THE PHENOMENON
OF DEATH

What is it like to die?

That is a question which humanity has been asking itself ever since there have been humans. Over the past few years, I have had the opportunity to raise this question before a sizable number of audiences. These groups have ranged from classes in psychology, philosophy, and sociology through church organizations, television audiences, and civic clubs to professional societies of medicine. On the basis of this exposure, I can safely say that this topic excites the most powerful of feelings from people of many emotional types and walks of life.

Yet, despite all this interest it remains true that it is very difficult for most of us to talk about death. There are at least two reasons for this. One of them is primarily psychological and cultural: The subject of death is taboo. We feel, perhaps only subconsciously, that to be in contact with death in any way, even indirectly, somehow confronts us with the prospect of our own deaths, draws our own deaths closer and makes them more real and

9

thinkable. For example, most medical students, myself included, have found that even the remote encounter with death which occurs upon one's first visit to the anatomical laboratories when entering medical school can evoke strong feelings of uneasiness. In my own case, the reason for this response now seems quite obvious. It has occurred to me in retrospect that it wasn't entirely concern for the person whose remains I saw there, although that feeling certainly figured, too. What I was seeing on that table was a symbol of my own mortality. In some way, if only pre-consciously, the thought must have been in my mind, "That will happen to me, too."

Likewise, talking about death can be seen on the psychological level as another way of approaching it indirectly. No doubt many people have the feeling that to talk about death at all is in effect to conjure it up mentally, to bring it closer in such a way that one has to face up to the inevitability of one's own eventual demise. So, to spare ourselves this psychological trauma, we decide just to try to avoid the topic as much as possible.

The second reason it is difficult to discuss death is more complicated, as it is rooted in the very nature of language itself. For the most part, the words of human language allude to things of which we have experience through our own physical senses. Death, though, is something which lies beyond the conscious experience of most of us because most of us have never been through it.

If we are to talk about death at all, then, we must avoid both social taboos and the deep-seated linguistic dilemmas which derive from our own inexperience. What we often end up doing is talking in euphemistic analogies. We compare death or dying with more pleasant things in our experience, things with which we are familiar.

Perhaps the most common analogy of this type is the comparison between death and sleep. Dying, we tell ourselves, is like going to sleep. This figure of speech occurs very commonly in everyday thought and language, as well as in the literature of many cultures and many ages. It was apparently quite common even in the time of the ancient Greeks. In *The Iliad*, for example, Homer calls sleep "death's sister," and Plato, in his dialogue *The Apology*, put the following words into the mouth of his teacher, Socrates, who has just been sentenced to death by an Athenian jury.

[Now, if death is only a dreamless sleep,] it must be a marvelous gain. I suppose that if anyone were told to pick out the night on which he slept so soundly as not even to dream, and then to compare it with all the other nights and days of his life, and then were told to say, after due consideration, how many better and happier days and nights than this he had spent in the course of his life—well, I think that . . . [anyone] would find these days and nights easy to count in comparison with the rest. If death is like this, then, I call it gain, because the whole of time, if you look at it in this way, can be regarded as no more than one single night.[1]

This same analogy is embedded in our own contemporary language. Consider the phrase "to put to sleep." If you present your dog to a veterinarian with the instruction to put him to sleep, you would normally mean something very different than you would upon taking your wife or husband to an anesthesiologist with the same words. Others prefer a different, but related analogy. Dying, they say, is like forgetting. When one dies, one forgets all one's woes; all one's painful and troubling memories are obliterated.

As old and as widespread as they may be, however, both the "sleeping" and the "forgetting" analogies are ultimately inadequate in so far as comforting us is concerned. Each is a different way of making the same assertion. Even though they tell us so in a somewhat more palatable way, both say, in effect, that death is simply the annihilation of conscious experience, forever. If this is so, then death really doesn't have any of the desirable features of sleeping and forgetting. Sleeping is a positive, desirable experience in life because waking follows it. A restful night's sleep makes the waking hours following it more pleasant and productive. If waking did not follow it, the benefits of sleep would not be possible. Similarly, annihilation of all conscious experience implies not only the obliteration of all painful memories, but of all pleasant ones, too. So upon analysis, neither analogy is close enough to give us any real comfort or hope in facing death.

There is another view, however, which disavows the notion that death is annihilation of consciousness. According to this other, perhaps more ancient tradition, some aspect of the human being survives even after the physical body ceases to function and is ultimately destroyed. This persistent aspect has been called by many names, among them psyche, soul, mind, spirit, self, being, and consciousness. By whatever name it is called, the notion that one passes into another realm of existence upon physical death is among the most venerable of human beliefs. There is a graveyard in Turkey which was used by Neanderthal men approximately 100,000 years ago. There, fossilized imprints have enabled archaeologists to discover that these ancient men buried their dead in biers of flowers, indicating that they perhaps saw death as an occasion of celebration—as a transition of the dead from this world to the next. Indeed, graves from very early sites all over the earth give evidence of the belief in human survival of bodily death.

In short, we are faced with two contrasting answers to our original question about the nature of death, both of ancient derivation, yet both widely held even today. Some say that death is annihilation of consciousness; others say with equal confidence that death is the passage of the soul or mind into another dimension of reality. In what follows I do not wish in any way to dismiss either answer. I simply wish to give a report on a search which I have personally undertaken.

13

During the past few years I have encountered a large number of persons who were involved in what I shall call "near-death experiences." I have met these persons in many ways. At first it was by coincidence. In 1965, when I was an undergraduate student studying philosophy at the University of Virginia, I met a man who was a clinical professor of psychiatry in the School of Medicine. I was struck from the beginning with his warmth, kindliness and humor. It came as a great surprise when I later learned a very interesting fact about him, namely, that he had been dead—not just once but on two occasions, about ten minutes apart—and that he had given a most fantastic account of what happened to him while he was "dead." I later heard him relate his story to a small group of interested students. At the time, I was most impressed, but since I had little background from which to judge such experiences, I "filed it away," both in my mind and in the form of a tape recording of his talk.

Some years later, after I had received my Ph.D. in philosophy, I was teaching in a university in eastern North Carolina. In one course I had my students read Plato's *Phaedo*, a work in which immortality is among the subjects discussed. In my lectures I had been emphasizing the other doctrines which Plato presents there and had not focused upon the discussion of life after death. After class one day a student stopped by to see me. He

14

asked whether we might discuss the subject of immortality. He had an interest in the subject because his grandmother had "died" during an operation and had recounted a very amazing experience. I asked him to tell me about it, and much to my surprise, he related almost the same series of events which I had heard the psychiatry professor describe some years before.

At this time my search for cases became a bit more active, and I began to include readings on the subject of human survival of biological death in my philosophy courses. However, I was careful not to mention the two death experiences in my courses. I adopted, in effect, a wait-and-see attitude. If such reports were fairly common, I thought, I would probably hear of more if I just brought up the general topic of survival in philosophical discussions, expressed a sympathetic attitude toward the question, and waited. To my amazement, I found that in almost every class of thirty or so students, at least one student would come to me afterwards and relate a personal near-death experience.

What has amazed me since the beginning of my interest are the great similarities in the reports, despite the fact that they come from people of highly varied religious, social, and educational backgrounds. By the time I entered medical school in 1972, I had collected a sizable number of these experiences and I began mentioning the informal study I had been doing to some of my medical acquaintances. Eventually, a friend of mine talked me into giving a report to a medical society, and other public talks followed. Again, I found that after every talk someone would come up to tell me of an experience of his own.

As I became more widely known for this interest, doctors began to refer to me persons whom they had resuscitated and who reported unusual experiences. Still others have written to me with reports after newspaper articles about my studies appeared.

At the present time, I know of approximately 150 cases of this phenomenon. The experiences which I have studied fall into three distinct categories:

(1) The experiences of persons who were resuscitated after having been thought, adjudged, or pronounced clinically dead by their doctors.

(2) The experiences of persons who, in the course of accidents or severe injury or illness, came very close to physical death.

(3) The experiences of persons who, as they died, told them to other people who were present. Later, these other people reported the content of the death experience to me.

From the vast amount of material that could be derived from 150 cases, selection obviously has occurred. Some of it has been purposeful. For example, although I have found reports of the third type to complement and to agree very well with experiences of the first two types, I have for the most part dropped them from consideration for two reasons. First, it helps to reduce the number of cases studied to a more manageable level, and second, it enables me to stick as close as possible to firsthand reports. Thus, I have interviewed in great detail some fifty persons upon whose experiences I am able to report. Of these, the cases of the first type (those in which an apparent clinical death actually occurs) are certainly more *dramatic* than those of the second type (in which only a close brush with death occurs). Indeed, whenever I have given public talks on this phenomenon, the "death" episodes have invariably drawn most of the interest. Accounts in the press have sometimes been written so as to suggest they are the *only* type of case with which I have dealt.

However, in selecting the cases to be presented in this book, I have avoided the temptation to dwell only on those cases in which a "death" event took place. For, as will become obvious, cases of the second type are not different from, but rather form a continuum with, cases of the first type. Also, though the near-death experiences themselves are remarkably similar, both the circumstances surrounding them and the persons describing them vary widely. Accordingly, I have tried to give a sample of experiences which adequately reflects this variation. With these qualifications in mind, let us now turn to a consideration of what may happen, as far as I have been able to discover, during the experience of dying.

[1]Plato, *The Last Days of Socrates*, trans. Hugh Tredennick (Baltimore: Penguin Books, 1959), p. 75.

2
THE EXPERIENCE
OF DYING

Despite the wide variation in the circumstances surrounding close calls with death and in the types of persons undergoing them, it remains true that there is a striking similarity among the accounts of the experiences themselves. In fact, the similarities among various reports are so great that one can easily pick out about fifteen separate elements which recur again and again in the mass of narratives that I have collected. On the basis of these points of likeness, let me now construct a brief, theoretically "ideal" or "complete" experience which embodies all of the common elements, in the order in which it is typical for them to occur.

A man is dying and, as he reaches the point of greatest physical distress, he hears himself pronounced dead by his doctor. He begins to hear an uncomfortable noise, a loud ringing or buzzing, and at the same time feels himself moving very rapidly through a long dark tunnel. After this, he suddenly finds himself outside of his own physical body, but still in the immediate physical environment, and he sees his own body from a distance, as though he is a spectator. He watches the resuscitation attempt from this unusual vantage point and is in a state of emotional upheaval.

After a while, he collects himself and becomes more accustomed to his odd condition. He notices that he still has a "body," but one of a very different nature and with very different powers from the physical body he has left behind. Soon other things begin to happen. Others come to meet and to help him. He glimpses the spirits of relatives and friends who have already died, and a loving, warm spirit of a kind he has never encountered before—a being of light—appears before him. This being asks him a question, nonverbally, to make him evaluate his life and helps him along by showing him a panoramic, instantaneous playback of the major events of his life. At some point he finds himself approaching some sort of barrier or border, apparently representing the limit between earthly life and the next life. Yet, he finds that he must go back to the earth, that the time for his death has not yet come. At this point he resists, for by now he is taken up with his experiences in the afterlife and does not want to return. He is overwhelmed by intense feelings of joy, love, and peace. Despite his attitude, though, he somehow reunites with his physical body and lives.

Later he tries to tell others, but he has trouble

doing so. In the first place, he can find no human words adequate to describe these unearthly episodes. He also finds that others scoff, so he stops telling other people. Still, the experience affects his life profoundly, especially his views about death and its relationship to life.

It is important to bear in mind that the above narrative is not meant to be a representation of any one person's experience. Rather, it is a "model," a composite of the common elements found in very many stories. I introduce it here only to give a preliminary, general idea of what a person who is dying may experience. Since it is an abstraction rather than an actual account, in the present chapter I will discuss in detail each common element, giving many examples.

Before doing that, however, a few facts need to be set out in order to put the remainder of my exposition of the experience of dying into the proper framework.

(1) Despite the striking similarities among various accounts, no two of them are precisely identical (though a few come remarkably close to it).

(2) I have found no one person who reports every single component of the composite experience. Very many have reported most of them (that is, eight or more of the fifteen or so) and a few have reported up to twelve.

(3) There is no one element of the composite

experience which every single person has reported to me, which crops up in every narrative. Nonetheless, a few of these elements come fairly close to being universal.

(4) There is not one component of my abstract model which has appeared in only one account. Each element has shown up in many separate stories.

(5) The order in which a dying person goes through the various stages briefly delineated above may vary from that given in my "theoretical model." To give one example, various persons have reported seeing the "being of light" before, or at the same time, they left their physical bodies, and not as in the "model," some time afterward. However, the order in which the stages occur in the model is a very typical order, and wide variations are unusual.

(6) How far into the hypothetical complete experience a dying person gets seems to depend on whether or not the person actually underwent an apparent clinical death, and if so, on how long he was in this state. In general, persons who were "dead" seem to report more florid, complete experiences than those who only came close to death, and those who were "dead" for a longer period go deeper than those who were "dead" for a shorter time.

(7) I have talked to a few people who were pronounced dead, resuscitated, and came back reporting none of these common elements. Indeed, they say that they don't remember anything at all about

their "deaths." Interestingly enough, I have talked with several persons who were actually adjudged clinically dead on separate occasions years apart, and reported experiencing nothing on one of the occasions, but having had quite involved experiences on the other.

(8) It must be emphasized that I am writing primarily about reports, accounts, or narratives, which other persons have given to me verbally during interviews. Thus, when I remark that a given element of the abstract, "complete" experience does not occur in a given account, I do not mean necessarily to imply that it did not happen to the person involved. I only mean that this person did not tell me that it did occur, or that it does not definitely come out in his account that he experienced it. Within this framework, then, let us look at some of the common stages and events of the experiences of dying.

Ineffability

The general understanding we have of language depends upon the existence of a broad community of common experience in which almost all of us participate. This fact creates an important difficulty which complicates all of the discussion which is to follow. The events which those who have come near death have lived through lie outside our community of experience, so one might well expect that they would have some linguistic difficulties in expressing what happened to them. In fact, this is precisely the case. The persons involved uniformly characterize their experiences as ineffable, that is, "inexpressible."

Many people have made remarks to the effect that, "There are just no words to express what I am trying to say," or "They just don't make adjectives and superlatives to describe this." One woman put this to me very succinctly when she said:

Now, there is a real problem for me as I'm trying to tell you this, because all the words I know are three-dimensional. As I was going through this, I kept thinking, "Well, when I was taking geometry, they always told me there were only three dimensions, and I always just accepted that. But they were wrong. There are more." And, of course, our world—the one we're living in now—*is* three-dimensional, but the next one definitely isn't. And that's why it's so hard to tell you this. I have to describe it to you in words that are three-dimensional. That's as close as I can get to it, but it's not really adequate. I can't really give you a complete picture.

Hearing The News

Numerous people have told of hearing their doctors or other spectators in effect pronounce them dead. One woman related to me that,

I was in the hospital, but they didn't know what was wrong with me. So Dr. James, my doctor, sent me downstairs to the radiologist for a liver scan so they could find out. First, they tested this drug they were going to use on my arm, since I had a lot of drug allergies. But there was no reaction, so they went ahead. When they used it this time, I arrested on them. I heard the radiologist who was working on me go over to the telephone, and I heard very clearly as he dialed it. I heard him say, "Dr. James, I've killed your patient, Mrs. Martin." And I knew I wasn't dead. I tried to move or to let them know, but I couldn't. When they were trying to resuscitate me, I could hear them telling how many c.c.'s of something to give me, but I didn't feel the needles going in. I felt nothing at all when they touched me.

In another case, a woman who had previously had several episodes of heart trouble was seized with a heart attack, during which she nearly lost her life. She says,

Suddenly, I was gripped by squeezing chest pains, just as though an iron band had been clamped quickly around the middle part of my chest and tightened. My husband and a friend of ours heard me fall and came running in to help me. I found myself in a deep blackness, and through it I heard my husband, as if he were at a great distance, saying, "This is it, this time!" And my thoughts were, "Yes, it is."

A young man who was thought dead following an automobile accident says, "I heard a woman who was there say, 'Is he dead?' and someone else said, 'Yeah, he's dead'."

Reports of this type accord quite well with what the doctors and others present remember. For example, one doctor told me,

A woman patient of mine had a cardiac arrest just before another surgeon and I were to operate on her. I was right there, and I saw her pupils dilate. We tried for some time to resuscitate her, but weren't having any success, so I thought she was gone. I told the other doctor who was working with me, "Let's try one more time and then we'll give up." This time, we got her heart beating, and she came around. Later I asked her what she remembered of her "death." She said she didn't remember much about it, except that she did hear me say, "Let's try one more time and then we'll give up."

Feelings of Peace and Quiet

Many people describe extremely pleasant feelings and sensations during the early stages of their experiences. After a severe head injury, one man's vital signs were undetectable. As he says,

At the point of injury there was a momentary flash of pain, but then all the pain vanished. I had the feeling of floating in a dark space. The day was bitterly cold, yet while I was in that blackness all I felt was warmth and the most

28

extreme comfort I have ever experienced. . . . I remember thinking, "I must be dead."

A woman who was resuscitated after a heart attack remarks,

I began to experience the most wonderful feelings. I couldn't feel a thing in the world except peace, comfort, ease—just quietness. I felt that all my troubles were gone, and I thought to myself, "Well how quiet and peaceful, and I don't hurt at all."

Another man recalls,

I just had a nice, great feeling of solitude and peace. . . . It was beautiful, and I was at such peace in my mind.

A man who "died" after wounds suffered in Viet Nam says that as he was hit he felt

A great attitude of relief. There was no pain, and I've never felt so relaxed. I was at ease and it was all good.

The Noise

In many cases, various unusual auditory sensations are reported to occur at or near death. Sometimes these are extremely unpleasant. A man who "died" for twenty minutes during an abdominal operation describes "a really bad buzzing noise coming from inside my head. It made me very uncomfortable. . . . . I'll never forget that noise." Another woman tells how as she lost consciousness she heard "a loud ringing. It could be described as a buzzing. And I was in a sort of whirling state." I have also heard this annoying sensation described as a loud click, a roaring, a banging, and as a "whistling sound, like the wind."

In other cases the auditory effects seem to take a more pleasant musical form. For example, a man who was revived after having been pronounced dead on arrival at the hospital recounts that during his death experience,

> I would hear what seemed to be bells tingling, a long way off, as if drifting through the wind. They sounded like Japanese wind bells. . . . That was the only sound I could hear at times.

A young woman who nearly died from internal bleeding associated with a blood clotting disorder says that at the moment she collapsed, "I began to hear music of some sort, a majestic, really beautiful sort of music."

The Dark Tunnel

Often concurrently with the occurrence of the noise, people have the sensation of being pulled very rapidly through a dark space of some kind. Many different words are used to describe this space. I have heard this space described as a cave, a well, a trough, an enclosure, a tunnel, a funnel, a vacuum, a void, a sewer, a valley, and a cylinder. Although people use different terminology here, it is clear that they are all trying to express some one idea. Let us look at two accounts in which the "tunnel" figures prominently.

This happened to me when I was a little boy— nine years old. That was twenty-seven years ago, but it was so striking that I have never forgotten it. One afternoon I became very sick, and they rushed me to the nearest hospital. When I arrived they decided they were going to have to put me to sleep, but why I don't know, because I was too young. Back in those days they used ether. They gave it to me by putting a cloth over my nose, and when they did, I was told afterwards, my heart stopped beating. I didn't know at that time that that was exactly what happened to me, but anyway when this happened I had an experience. Well, the first thing that happened— now I am going to describe it just the way I felt—was that I had this ringing noise brrrrr-nnnnng-brrrrrnnnnng-brrrrrnnnnng, very rhythmic. Then I was moving through this—you're going to think this is weird—through this long dark place. It seemed like a sewer or something. I just can't describe it to you. I was moving, beating all the time with this noise, this ringing noise.

Another informant states:

I had a very bad allergic reaction to a local anesthetic, and I just quit breathing—I had a re-

spiratory arrest. The first thing that happened—
it was real quick—was that I went through this
dark, black vacuum at super speed. You could
compare it to a tunnel, I guess. I felt like I was
riding on a roller coaster train at an amusement
park, going through this tunnel at a tremendous
speed.

During a severe illness, a man came so near death
that his pupils dilated and his body was growing
cold. He says,

I was in an utterly black, dark void. It is very
difficult to explain, but I felt as if I were moving
in a vacuum, just through blackness. Yet, I was
quite conscious. It was like being in a cylinder
which had no air in it. It was a feeling of limbo,
of being half-way here, and half-way somewhere
else.

A man who "died" several times after severe
burns and fall injuries says,

I stayed in shock for about a week, and during
that time all of a sudden I just escaped into this
dark void. It seemed that I stayed there for a
long time just floating and tumbling through
space. . . . I was so taken up with this void that I
just didn't think of anything else.

Before the time of his experience, which took
place when he was a child, one man had had a fear
of the dark. Yet, when his heart stopped beating
from internal injuries incurred in a bicycle accident,

I had the feeling that I was moving through a deep, very dark valley. The darkness was so deep and impenetrable that I could see absolutely nothing but this was the most wonderful, worry-free experience you can imagine.

In another case, a woman had had peritonitis, and relates,

My doctor had already called my brother and sister in to see me for the last time. The nurse gave me a shot to help me die more easily. The things around me in the hospital began to get further and further away. As they receded, I entered head first into a narrow and very, very dark passageway. I seemed to just fit inside of it. I began to slide down, down, down.

One woman, who was near death following a traffic accident, drew a parallel from a television show.

There was a feeling of utter peace and quiet, no fear at all, and I found myself in a tunnel—a tunnel of concentric circles. Shortly after that, I saw a T.V. program called *The Time Tunnel*, where people go back in time through this spiralling tunnel. Well, that's the closest thing to it that I can think of.

A man who came very near death drew a somewhat different parallel, one from his religious background. He says,

Suddenly, I was in a very dark, very deep valley. It was as though there was a pathway, almost a road, through the valley, and I was going down the path. . . . Later, after I was well, the thought came to me, "Well, now I know what the Bible means by 'the valley of the shadow of death,' because I've been there."

Out Of The Body

It is a truism that most of us, most of the time, identify ourselves with our physical bodies. We grant, of course, that we have "minds," too. But to most people our "minds" seem much more ephemeral than our bodies. The "mind," after all, might be no more than the effect of the electrical and chemical activity which takes place in the brain, which is a part of the physical body. For many people it is an impossible task even to conceive of what it would be like to exist in any other way than in the physical body to which they are accustomed.

Prior to their experiences, the persons I have interviewed were not, as a group, any different from the average person with respect to this attitude. That is why, after his rapid passage through the dark tunnel, a dying person often has such an overwhelming surprise. For, at this point he may find himself looking upon his own physical body from a point outside of it, as though he were "a spectator" or "a third person in the room" or watching figures and events "onstage in a play" or "in

34

a movie." Let us look now at portions of some accounts in which these uncanny out-of-the-body episodes are described.

I was seventeen years old and my brother and I were working at an amusement park. One afternoon, we decided to go swimming, and there were quite a few of the other young people who went in with us. Someone said, "Let's swim across the lake." I had done that on numerous occasions, but that day for some reason, I went down, almost in the middle of the lake. . . . I kept bobbling up and down, and all of a sudden, it felt as though I were away from my body, away from everybody, in space by myself. Although I was stable, staying at the same level, I saw my body in the water about three or four feet away, bobbling up and down. I viewed my body from the back and slightly to the right side. I still felt as though I had an entire body form, even while I was outside my body. I had an airy feeling that's almost indescribable. I felt like a feather.

A woman recalls,

About a year ago, I was admitted to the hospital with heart trouble, and the next morning, lying in the hospital bed, I began to have a very severe pain in my chest. I pushed the button beside the bed to call for the nurses, and they came in and started working on me. I was quite uncomfortable lying on my back so I turned over, and as I did I quit breathing and my heart stopped beating. Just then, I heard the nurses shout, "Code pink! Code pink!" As they were saying this, I could feel myself moving out of my body and sliding down between the mattress and the rail on the side of the bed—actually it seemed as if I went *through* the rail—on down to the floor. Then, I started rising upward, slowly. On my way up, I saw more nurses come running into the room—there must have been a dozen of them. My doctor happened to be making his rounds in the hospital so they called him and I saw him come in, too. I thought, "I wonder what he's doing here." I drifted on up past the light fixture—I saw it from the side and very distinctly—and then I stopped, floating right below the ceiling, looking down. I felt almost as though I were a piece of paper that someone had blown up to the ceiling.

I watched them reviving me from up there! My body was lying down there stretched out on the bed, in plain view, and they were all standing around it. I heard one nurse say, "Oh, my God! She's gone!", while another one leaned down to give me mouth-to-mouth resuscitation. I was looking at the *back* of her head while she did this. I'll never forget the way her hair looked; it was cut kind of short. Just then, I saw them roll this machine in there, and they put the shocks on my chest. When they did, I saw my whole body just jump right up off the bed, and I heard every bone in my body crack and pop. It was the most awful thing!

As I saw them below beating on my chest and rubbing my arms and legs, I thought, "Why are they going to so much trouble? I'm just fine now."

A young informant states,

It was about two years ago, and I had just turned nineteen. I was driving a friend of mine home in my car, and as I got to this particular intersection downtown, I stopped and looked both ways, but I didn't see a thing coming. I pulled on out into the intersection and as I did I heard my friend yell at the top of his voice. When I looked I saw a blinding light, the headlights of a car that was speeding towards us. I heard this awful sound—the side of the car being crushed in—and there was just an instant during which I seemed to be going through a darkness, an enclosed space. It was very quick. Then, I was sort of floating about five feet above the street, about five yards away from the car, I'd say, and I heard the echo of the crash dying away. I saw people come running up and crowding around the car, and I saw my friend get out of the car, obviously in shock. I could see my own body in the wreckage among all those people, and could see them trying to get it out. My legs were all twisted and there was blood all over the place.

As one might well imagine, some unparalleled thoughts and feelings run through the minds of persons who find themselves in this predicament. Many people find the notion of being out of their bodies so unthinkable that, even as they are experiencing it, they feel conceptually quite confused about the whole thing and do not link it with death for a considerable time. They wonder what is happening to them; why can they suddenly see themselves from a distance, as though a spectator?

Emotional responses to this strange state vary widely. Most people report, at first, a desperate desire to get back into their bodies but they do not have the faintest idea about how to proceed. Others recall that they were very afraid, almost panicky. Some, however, report more positive reactions to their plight, as in this account:

I became very seriously ill, and the doctor put me in the hospital. This one morning a solid gray mist gathered around me, and I left my body. I had a floating sensation as I felt myself get out of my body, and I looked back and I could see myself on the bed below and there was no fear. It was quiet—very peaceful and serene. I was not in the least bit upset or frightened. It was just a tranquil feeling, and it was something which I didn't dread. I felt that maybe I was dying, and I felt that if I did not get back to my body, I would be dead, gone.

Just as strikingly variable are the attitudes which different persons take to the bodies which they have left behind. It is common for a person to report feelings of concern for his body. One young woman, who was a nursing student at the time of her experience, expresses an understandable fear.

This is sort of funny, I know, but in nursing school they had tried to drill it into us that we ought to donate our bodies to science. Well, all through this, as I watched them trying to start my breathing again, I kept thinking, "I don't want them to use that body as a cadaver."

I have heard two other persons express exactly this same concern when they found themselves out of their bodies. Interestingly enough, both of them were also in the medical profession—one a physician, the other a nurse.

In another case, this concern took the form of regret. A man's heart stopped beating following a fall in which his body was badly mangled, and he recalls,

At one time—now, I know I was lying on the bed there—but I could actually see the bed and the doctor working on me. I couldn't understand it, but I looked at my own body lying there on the bed. And I felt real bad when I looked at my body and saw how badly it was messed up.

Several persons have told me of having feelings of unfamiliarity toward their bodies, as in this rather striking passage.

Boy, I sure didn't realize that I looked like that! You know, I'm only used to seeing myself in pictures or from the front in a mirror, and both of those look *flat*. But all of a sudden there I—or my body—was and I could see it. I could definitely see it, full view, from about five feet away. It took me a few moments to recognize myself.

In one account, this feeling of unfamiliarity took a rather extreme and humorous form. One man, a physician, tells how during his clinical "death" he was beside the bed looking at his own cadaver, which by then had turned the ash gray color assumed by bodies after death. Desperate and confused, he was trying to decide what to do. He tentatively decided just to go away, as he was feeling very uneasy. As a youngster he had been told ghost stories by his grandfather and, paradoxically, he "didn't like being around this thing that looked like a dead body—even if it was me!"

At the other extreme, some have told me that they had no particular feelings at all toward their bodies. One woman, for example, had a heart attack and felt certain she was dying. She felt herself being pulled through darkness out of her body and moving rapidly away. She says,

> I didn't look back at my body at all. Oh, I knew it was there, all right, and I could've seen it had I looked. But I didn't want to look, not in the least, because I knew that I had done my best in my life, and I was turning my attention now to this other realm of things. I felt that to look back at my body would be to look back at the past, and I was determined not to do that.

Similarly, a girl whose out-of-body experience took place after a wreck in which she sustained severe injuries says,

> I could see my own body all tangled up in the car amongst all the people who had gathered around, but, you know, I had no feelings for it

whatsoever. It was like it was a completely different human, or maybe even just an object. . . . I knew it was my body but I had no feelings for it.

Despite the eeriness of the disembodied state, the situation has been thrust upon the dying person so suddenly that it may take some time before the significance of what he is experiencing dawns upon him. He may be out of his body for some time, desperately trying to sort out all the things that are happening to him and that are racing through his mind, before he realizes that he is dying, or even dead.

When this realization comes, it may arrive with powerful emotional force, and provoke startling thoughts. One woman remembers thinking, "Oh, I'm dead! How lovely!"

A man states that the thought came to him, "This must be what they call 'death'." Even when this realization comes, it may be accompanied by bafflement and even a certain refusal to accept one's state. One man, for example, remembers reflecting upon the Biblical promise of "three score and ten" years, and protesting that he had had "just barely one score." A young woman gave a very impressive account of such feelings when she told me that,

I thought I was dead, and I wasn't sorry that I was dead, but I just couldn't figure out where I was supposed to go. My thought and my consciousness were just like they are in life, but I just couldn't figure all this out. I kept thinking, "Where am I going to go? What am I going to do?" and "My God, I'm dead! I can't believe it!" Because you never really believe, I don't think, fully that you're going to die. It's always something that's going to happen to the other person, and although you know it you really never believe it deep down. . . . And so I decided I was just going to wait until all the excitement died down and they carried my body away, and try to see if I could figure out where to go from there.

In one or two cases I have studied, dying persons whose souls, minds, consciousnesses (or whatever you want to label them) were released from their bodies say that they didn't feel that, after release, they were in any kind of "body" at all. They felt as though they were "pure" consciousness. One man relates that during his experience he felt as though he were "able to see everything around me —including my whole body as it lay on the bed— without occupying any space," that is, as if he were a point of consciousness. A few others say that they can't really remember whether or not they were in any kind of "body" after getting out of their physical one, because they were so taken up with the events around them.

Far and away the majority of my subjects, however, report that they did find themselves in another body upon release from the physical one. Immediately, though, we are into an area with which it is extremely difficult to deal. This "new body" is one of the two or three aspects of death experiences in which the inadequacy of human language presents the greatest obstacles. Almost everyone who has told me of this "body" has at some point become frustrated and said, "I can't describe it," or made some remark to the same effect.

Nonetheless, the accounts of this body bear a strong resemblance to one another. Thus, although different individuals use different words and draw different analogies, these varying modes of expression do seem to fall very much within the same arena. The various reports are also in very decided agreement about the general properties and characteristics of the new body. So, to adopt a term for it which will sum up its properties fairly well, and which has been used by a couple of my subjects, I shall henceforth call it the "spiritual body."

Dying persons are likely first to become aware of their spiritual bodies in the guise of their limitations. They find, when out of their physical bodies, that although they may try desperately to tell others of their plight, no one seems to hear them. This is illustrated very well in this excerpt from the story of a woman who suffered a respiratory arrest and was carried to the emergency room, where a resuscitation attempt was made.

> I saw them resuscitating me. It was really strange. I wasn't very high; it was almost like I was on a pedestal, but not above them to any

great extent, just maybe looking over them. I tried talking to them but nobody could hear me, nobody would listen to me.

To complicate the fact that he is apparently inaudible to people around him, the person in a spiritual body soon finds that he is also invisible to others. The medical personnel or others congregating around his physical body may look straight towards where he is, in his spiritual body, without giving the slightest sign of ever seeing him. His spiritual body also lacks solidity; physical objects in the environment appear to move through it with ease, and he is unable to get a grip on any object or person he tries to touch.

The doctors and nurses were pounding on my body to try to get IV's started and to get me back, and I kept trying to tell them, "Leave me alone. All I want is to be left alone. Quit pounding on me." But they didn't hear me. So I tried to move their hands to keep them from beating on my body, but nothing would happen. I couldn't get anywhere. It was like—I don't really know what happened, but I couldn't move their hands. It looked like I was touching their hands and I tried to move them—yet when I would give it the stroke, their hands were still there. I don't know whether my hand was going through it, around it, or what. I didn't feel any pressure against their hands when I was trying to move them.

Or,

People were walking up from all directions to get to the wreck. I could see them, and I was in the middle of a very narrow walkway. Anyway, as they came by they wouldn't seem to notice me. They would just keep walking with their eyes straight ahead. As they came real close, I would try to turn around, to get out of their way, but they would just walk *through* me.

Further, it is invariably reported that this spiritual body is also weightless. Most first notice this when, as in some of the excerpts given above, they find themselves floating right up to the ceiling of the room, or into the air. Many describe a "floating sensation," "a feeling of weightlessness," or a "drifting feeling" in association with their new bodies.

Normally, while in our physical bodies we have many modes of perception which tell us where our bodies and their various parts are in space at any given moment and whether they are moving. Vision and the sense of equilibrium are important in this respect, of course, but there is another related sense. Kinesthesia is our sense of motion or tension in our tendons, joints, and muscles. We are not usually aware of the sensations coming to us through our kinesthetic sense because our perception of it has become dulled through almost constant use. I suspect, however, that if it were suddenly to be cut off, one would immediately notice its absence. And, in fact, quite a few persons have commented to me that they were aware of the lack of the physical sensations of body weight, movement, and position sense while in their spiritual bodies.

These characteristics of the spiritual body which at first seem to be limitations can, with equal validity, be looked upon as the absence of limitations. Think of it this way: A person in the spiritual body is in a privileged position in relation to the other persons around him. He can see and hear them, but they can't see or hear him. (Many a spy would consider this an enviable condition.) Likewise, though the doorknob seems to go through his hand when he touches it, it really doesn't matter anyway, because he soon finds that he can just *go through* the door. Travel, once one gets the hang of it, is apparently exceptionally easy in this state. Physical objects present no barrier, and movement from one place to another can be extremely rapid, almost instantaneous.

Furthermore, despite its lack of perceptibility to people in physical bodies, all who have experienced it are in agreement that the spiritual body is nonetheless *something*, impossible to describe though it may be. It is agreed that the spiritual body has a form or shape (sometimes a globular or an amorphous cloud, but also sometimes essentially the same shape as the physical body) and even parts (projections or surfaces analogous to arms, legs, a head, etc.). Even when its shape is reported as being generally roundish in configuration, it is often said to have ends, a definite top and bottom, and even the "parts" just mentioned.

I have heard this new body described in many different terms, but one may readily see that much the same idea is being formulated in each case. Words and phrases which have been used by various subjects include a mist, a cloud, smoke-like, a vapor, transparent, a cloud of colors, wispy, an energy pattern and others which express similar meanings.

Finally, almost everyone remarks upon the *timelessness* of this out-of-body state. Many say that although they must describe their interlude in the spiritual body in temporal terms (since human language is temporal), time was not really an element of their experience as it is in physical life. Here are passages from five interviews in which some of these fantastic aspects of existence in the spiritual body are reported first-hand.

(1) I lost control of my car on a curve, and the car left the road and went into the air, and I remember seeing the blue sky and saw that the car was going down into a ditch. At the time the car left the road, I said to myself "I'm in an accident." At that point, I kind of lost my sense of time, and I lost my physical reality as far as my body is concerned—I lost touch with my body. My being or my self or my spirit, or whatever you would like to label it—I could sort of feel it rise out of me, out through my head.

47

And it wasn't anything that hurt, it was just sort of like a lifting and it being above me. . . .

[My "being"] felt as if it had a *density* to it, almost, but not a physical density—kind of like, I don't know, waves or something, I guess: Nothing really physical, almost as if it were charged, if you'd like to call it that. But it felt as if it had something to it. . . . It was small, and it felt as if it were sort of circular, with no rigid outlines to it. You could liken it to a cloud. . . . It almost seemed as if it were in its own encasement. . . .

As it went out of my body, it seemed that a large end left first, and the small end last. . . . It was a very light feeling—very. There was no strain on my [physical] body; the feeling was totally separate. My body had no weight. . . .

The most striking point of the whole experience was the moment when my being was suspended above the front part of my head. It was almost like it was trying to decide whether it wanted to leave or to stay. It seemed then as though time were standing still. At the first and the last of the accident, everything moved so fast, but at this one particular time, sort of in between, as my being was suspended above me and the car was going over the embankment, it seemed that it took the car a long time to get there, and in that time I really wasn't too involved with the car or the accident or my own body—only with my mind. . . .

My being had no physical characteristics, but I have to describe it with physical terms. I could describe it in so many ways, in so many words, but none of them would be exactly right. It's so hard to describe.

48

Finally, the car did hit the ground and it rolled over, but my only injuries were a sprained neck and a bruised foot.

(2) [When I came out of the physical body] it was like I did come out of my body and go into something else. I didn't think I was just nothing. It was another body . . . but not another regular human body. It's a little bit different. It was not exactly like a human body, but it wasn't any big glob of matter, either. It had form to it, but no colors. And I know I still had something you could call hands.

I can't describe it. I was more fascinated with everything around me—seeing my own body there, and all—so I didn't think about the type of body I was in. And all this seemed to go so quickly. Time wasn't really an element—and yet it was. Things seem to go faster after you get out of your body.

(3) I remember being wheeled into the operating room and the next few hours were the critical period. During that time, I kept getting in and out of my physical body, and I could see it from directly above. But, while I did, I was still in a body—not a physical body, but something I can best describe as an energy pattern. If I had to put it into words, I would say that it was transparent, a spiritual as opposed to a material being. Yet, it definitely had different parts.

(4) When my heart stopped beating . . . I felt like I was a round ball and almost maybe like I might have been a little sphere—like a B-B—on the inside of this round ball. I just can't describe it to you.

(5) I was out of my body looking at it from about ten yards away, but I was still thinking, just like in physical life. And *where* I was thinking was about at my normal bodily height. I wasn't in a body, as such. I could feel something, some kind of a—like a capsule, or something, like a clear form. I couldn't really see it; it was like it was transparent, but not really. It was like I was just there—an energy, maybe, sort of like just a little ball of energy. And I really wasn't aware of any bodily sensation—temperature, or anything like that.

In their accounts, others have briefly mentioned the likeness of shape between their physical bodies and their new ones. One woman told me that while out of her body, "I still felt an entire body form, legs, arms, everything—even while I was weightless." A lady who watched the resuscitation attempt on her body from a point just below the ceiling says, "I was still in a body. I was stretched out and looking down. I moved my legs and noticed that one of them felt warmer than the other one."

Just as movement is unimpeded in this spiritual state, so, some recall, is thought. Over and over, I have been told that once they became accustomed to their new situation, people undergoing this experience began to think more lucidly and rapidly than in physical existence. For example, one man told me that while he was "dead,"

Things that are not possible now, are then. Your mind is so clear. It's so nice. My mind just took everything down and worked everything out for me the first time, without having to go through it more than once. After a while everything I was experiencing got to where it meant something to me in some way.

Perception in the new body is both like and unlike perception in the physical body. In some ways, the spiritual form is more limited. As we saw, kinesthesia, as such, is absent. In a couple of instances, persons have reported that they had no sensation of temperature, while in most cases feelings of comfortable "warmth" are reported. No one among all of my cases has reported any odors or tastes while out of their physical bodies.

On the other hand, senses which correspond to the physical senses of vision and of hearing are very definitely intact in the spiritual body, and seem actually heightened and more perfect than they are in physical life. One man says that while he was "dead" his vision seemed incredibly more powerful and, in his words, "I just can't understand how I could see so far." A woman who recalled this experience notes, "It seemed as if this spiritual sense had no limitations, as if I could look anywhere and everywhere." This phenomenon is described very graphically in this portion of an interview with a woman who was out of her body following an accident.

There was a lot of action going on, and people running around the ambulance. And whenever I would look at a person to wonder what they were thinking, it was like a zoom-up, exactly like through a zoom lens, and I was there. But it seemed that part of me—I'll call it my mind—was still where I had been, several yards away from my body. When I wanted to see someone at a distance, it seemed like part of me, kind of like a tracer, would go to that person. And it seemed to me at the time that if something happened anyplace in the world that I could just be there.

"Hearing" in the spiritual state can apparently be called so only by analogy, and most say that they do not really hear physical voices or sounds. Rather, they seem to pick up the thoughts of persons around them, and, as we shall see later, this same kind of direct transfer of thoughts can play an important role in the late stages of death experiences.

As one lady put it,

I could see people all around, and I could understand what they were saying. I didn't hear them, audibly, like I'm hearing you. It was more like knowing what they were thinking, exactly what they were thinking, but only in my mind, not in their actual vocabulary. I would catch it the second before they opened their mouths to speak.

Finally, on the basis of one unique and very interesting report, it would appear that even severe damage to the physical body in no way adversely affects the spiritual one. In this case, a man lost the better part of his leg in the accident that resulted in his clinical death. He knew this, because he saw his damaged body clearly, from a distance, as the doctor worked on it. Yet, while he was out of his body,

I could feel my body, and it was whole. I know that. I felt whole, and I felt that all of me was there, though it wasn't.

In this disembodied state, then, a person is cut off from others. He can see other people and understand their thoughts completely, but they are able neither to see nor to hear him. Communication with other human beings is effectively cut off, even through the sense of touch, since his spiritual body lacks solidity. Thus, it is not surprising that after a time in this state profound feelings of isolation and loneliness set in. As one man put it, he could see everything around him in the hospital —all the doctors, nurses, and other personnel going about their tasks. Yet, he could not communicate with them in any way, so "I was desperately alone."

Many others have described to me the intense feelings of loneliness which overcome them at this point.

My experience, all the things that I was going through, were so beautiful, but just indescribable. I wanted others to be there with me to see it, too, and I had the feeling that I would never be able to describe to anyone what I was seeing. I had the feeling of being lonesome because I wanted somebody to be there to experience it with me. But I knew nobody else could be there. I felt that I was in a private world at that time. I really felt a fit of depression then.

Or,

I was unable to touch anything, unable to communicate with any of the people around. It is an awesome, lonely feeling, a feeling of complete isolation. I knew that I was completely alone, by myself.

And again,

I was just amazed. I couldn't believe that it was happening. I wasn't really concerned or worried like "Oh, no, I'm dead and my parents are left behind and they'll be sad and I'll never see them again." Nothing like that ever entered my mind.

I was aware the whole time of being alone, though, very alone—almost like I was a visitor from someplace else. It was like all relations were cut. I know—it was like there was no love or anything. Everything was just so—technical. I don't understand, really.

The dying person's feelings of loneliness are soon dispelled, however, as he gets deeper into his near death experience. For, at some point, others come to him to give him aid in the transition he is undergoing. These may take the form of other spirits, often those of deceased relatives or friends the individual had known while he was alive. In a greater number of instances, among those I interviewed, a spiritual being of a much different character appears. In the next few sections we will look at such encounters.

Meeting Others

Quite a few have told me that at some point while they were dying—sometimes early in the experience, sometimes only after other events had taken place—they became aware of the presence of other spiritual beings in their vicinity, beings who apparently were there to ease them through their transition into death, or, in two cases, to tell them that their time to die had not yet come and that they must return to their physical bodies.

I had this experience when I was giving birth to a child. The delivery was very difficult, and I lost a lot of blood. The doctor gave me up, and told my relatives that I was dying. However, I was quite alert through the whole thing, and even as I heard him saying this I felt myself coming to. As I did, I realized that all these people were there, almost in multitudes it seems, hovering around the ceiling of the room. They were all people I had known in my past life, but who had passed on before. I recognized my grandmother and a girl I had known when I was in school, and many other relatives and friends. It seems that I mainly saw their faces and felt their presence. They all seemed pleased. It was a very happy occasion, and I felt that they had come to protect or to guide me. It was almost as if I were coming home, and they were there to greet or to welcome me. All this time, I had the feeling of everything light and beautiful. It was a beautiful and glorious moment.

One man remembers:

Several weeks before I nearly died, a good friend of mine, Bob, had been killed. Now the moment I got out of my body I had the feeling that Bob was standing there, right next to me. I could see him in my mind and felt like he was there, but it was strange. I didn't see him as his physical body. I could see things, but not in the physical form, yet just as clearly, his looks, everything. Does that make sense? He was there but he didn't have a physical body. It was kind of like a clear body, and I could sense every part of it—arms, legs, and so on—but I wasn't *seeing* it physically. I didn't think about it being odd at the time because I didn't really need to see him with my eyes. I didn't have eyes, anyway.

I kept asking him, "Bob, where do I go now? What has happened? Am I dead or not?" And he never answered me, never said a word. But, often, while I was in the hospital, he would be there, and I would ask him again, "What's going on?", but never any answer. And then the day the doctors said, "He's going to live," he left. I didn't see him again and didn't feel his presence. It was almost as though he were waiting until I passed that final frontier and then he would tell me, would give me the details on what was going on.

In other cases, the spirits people encounter are not persons whom they knew in physical life. One woman told of seeing during her out-of-body experience not only her own transparent spiritual body but also another one, that of another person who had died very recently. She did not know who this person was, but made the very interesting remark that "I did not see this person, this spirit, as having any particular *age*, at all. I didn't even have any sense of time myself."

In a very few instances, people have come to believe that the beings they encountered were their "guardian spirits." One man was told by such a spirit that, "I have helped you through this stage of your existence, but now I am going to turn you over to others." A woman told me that as she was leaving her body she detected the presence of two other spiritual beings there, and that they identified themselves as her "spiritual helpers."

In two very similar cases, persons told me of hearing a voice which told them that they were not dead yet, but that they must go back. As one of them tells it,

> I heard a voice, not a man's voice, but like a hearing beyond the physical senses, telling me what I had to do—go back—and I felt no fear of getting back into my physical body.

Finally, the spiritual beings may take a somewhat more amorphous form.

While I was dead, in this void, I talked to people—and yet, I really couldn't say that I talked to any *bodily* people. Yet, I had the feeling that there were people around me, and I could feel their presence, and could feel them moving, though I could never see anyone. Every now and then, I would talk with one of them, but I couldn't see them. And whenever I wondered what was going on, I would always get a thought back from one of them, that everything was all right, that I was dying but would be fine. So, my condition never worried me. I always got an answer back for every question that I asked. They didn't leave my mind void.

The Being Of Light

What is perhaps the most incredible common element in the accounts I have studied, and is certainly the element which has the most profound effect upon the individual, is the encounter with a very bright light. Typically, at its first appearance this light is dim, but it rapidly gets brighter until it reaches an unearthly brilliance. Yet, even though this light (usually said to be white or "clear") is of an indescribable brilliance, many make the specific point that it does not in any way hurt their eyes, or dazzle them, or keep them from seeing other things around them (perhaps because at this point they don't have physical "eyes" to be dazzled).

Despite the light's unusual manifestation, however, not one person has expressed any doubt whatsoever that it was a being, a being of light. Not only that, it is a personal being. It has a very definite personality. The love and the warmth which emanate from this being to the dying person are utterly beyond words, and he feels completely surrounded by it and taken up in it, completely at ease and accepted in the presence of this being. He senses an irresistible magnetic attraction to this light. He is ineluctably drawn to it.

Interestingly, while the above description of the being of light is utterly invariable, the identification of the being varies from individual to individual and seems to be largely a function of the religious background, training, or beliefs of the person involved. Thus, most of those who are Christians in training or belief identify the light as Christ and sometimes draw Biblical parallels in support of their interpretation. A Jewish man and woman identified the light as an "angel." It was clear, though, in both cases, that the subjects did not mean to imply that the being had wings, played a harp, or even had a human shape or appearance. There was only the light. What each was trying to get across was that they took the being to be an emissary, or a guide. A man who had had no religious beliefs or training at all prior to his experience simply identified what he saw as "a being of light." The same label was used by one lady of the Christian faith, who apparently did not feel any compulsion at all to call the light "Christ."

Shortly after its appearance, the being begins to communicate with the person who is passing over. Notably, this communication is of the same direct kind which we encountered earlier in the description of how a person in the spiritual body may "pick up the thoughts" of those around him. For, here again, people claim that they did not hear any physical voice or sounds coming from the being, nor did they respond to the being through audible sounds. Rather, it is reported that direct, unimpeded transfer of thoughts takes place, and in such a clear way that there is no possibility whatsoever either of misunderstanding or of lying to the light.

Furthermore, this unimpeded exchange does not even take place in the native language of the person. Yet, he understands perfectly and is instantaneously aware. He cannot even translate the thoughts and exchanges which took place while he was near death into the human language which he must speak now, after his resuscitation.

The next step of the experience clearly illustrates the difficulty of translating from this unspoken language. The being almost immediately directs a certain thought to the person into whose presence it has come so dramatically. Usually the persons with whom I have talked try to formulate the thought into a question. Among the translations I have heard are: "Are you prepared to die?", "Are you ready to die?", "What have you done with your life to show me?", and "What have you done with your life that is sufficient?" The first two formulations which stress "preparation," might at first seem to have a different sense from the second pair, which emphasize "accomplishment." However, some support for my own feeling that everyone is trying to express the same thought comes from the narrative of one woman who put it this way:

The first thing he said to me was, that he kind of asked me if I was ready to die, or what I had done with my life that I wanted to show him.

Furthermore, even in the case of more unusual ways of phrasing the "question," it turns out, upon elucidation, to have much the same force. For example, one man told me that during his "death,"

The voice asked me a question: "Is it worth it?" And what it meant was, did the kind of life I had been leading up to that point seem worthwhile to me then, knowing what I then knew.

Incidentally, all insist that this question, ultimate and profound as it may be in its emotional impact, is not at all asked in condemnation. The being, all seem to agree, does not direct the question to them to accuse or to threaten them, for they still feel the total love and acceptance coming from the light, no matter what their answer may be. Rather, the point of the question seems to be to make them think about their lives, to draw them

61

out. It is, if you will, a Socratic question, one asked
not to acquire information but to help the person
who is being asked to proceed along the path to the
truth by himself. Let us look at some firsthand
accounts of this fantastic being.

(1) I heard the doctors say that I was dead,
and that's when I began to feel as though I were
tumbling, actually kind of floating, through this
blackness, which was some kind of enclosure.
There are not really words to describe this.
Everything was very black, except that, way off
from me, I could see this light. It was a very,
very brilliant light, but not too large at first. It
grew larger as I came nearer and nearer to it.

I was trying to get to that light at the end, because I felt that it was Christ, and I was trying to
reach that point. It was not a frightening experience. It was more or less a pleasant thing.
For immediately, being a Christian, I had con-
nected the light with Christ, who said, "I am the
light of the world." I said to myself, "If this is
it, if I am to die, then I know who waits for me
at the end, there in that light."

(2) I got up and walked into the hall to go get
a drink, and it was at that point, as they found
out later, that my appendix ruptured. I became
very weak, and I fell down. I began to feel a sort
of drifting, a movement of my real being in and
out of my body, and to hear beautiful music. I
floated on down the hall and out the door onto
the screened-in porch. There, it almost seemed
that clouds, a pink mist really, began to gather
around me, and then I floated right straight on
through the screen, just as though it weren't

there, and up into this pure crystal clear light, an illuminating white light. It was beautiful and so bright, so radiant, but it didn't hurt my eyes. It's not any kind of light you can describe on earth. I didn't actually see a person in this light, and yet it has a special identity, it definitely does. It is a light of perfect understanding and perfect love.

The thought came to my mind, "Lovest thou me?" This was not exactly in the form of a question, but I guess the connotation of what the light said was, "If you do love me, go back and complete what you began in your life." And all during this time, I felt as though I were surrounded by an overwhelming love and compassion.

(3) I knew I was dying and that there was nothing I could do about it, because no one could hear me. . . . I was out of my body, there's no doubt about it, because I could see my own body there on the operating room table. My soul was out! All this made me feel very bad at first, but then, this really bright light came. It did seem that it was a little dim at first, but then it was this huge beam. It was just a tremendous amount of light, nothing like a big bright flashlight, it was just too much light. And it gave off heat to me; I felt a warm sensation.

It was a bright yellowish white—more white. It was tremendously bright; I just can't describe it. It seemed that it covered everything, yet it didn't prevent me from seeing everything around me—the operating room, the doctors and nurses, everything. I could see clearly, and it wasn't blinding.

At first, when the light came, I wasn't sure what was happening, but then, it asked, it kind of asked me if I was ready to die. It was like talking to a person, but a person wasn't there. The light's what was talking to me, but in a *voice*.

Now, I think that the voice that was talking to me actually realized that I wasn't ready to die. You know, it was just kind of testing me more than anything else. Yet, from the moment the light spoke to me, I felt really good—secure and loved. The love which came from it is just unimaginable, indescribable. It was a fun person to be with! And it had a sense of humor, too—definitely!

The Review

The initial appearance of the being of light and his probing, non-verbal questions are the prelude to a moment of startling intensity during which the being presents to the person a panoramic review of his life. It is often obvious that the being can see the individual's whole life displayed and that he doesn't himself need information. His only intention is to provoke reflection.

This review can only be described in terms of memory, since that is the closest familiar phenomenon to it, but it has characteristics which set it apart from any normal type of remembering. First of all, it is extraordinarily rapid. The memories, when they are described in temporal terms, are said to follow one another swiftly, in chronological order. Others recall no awareness of temporal order at all. The remembrance was instantaneous; everything appeared at once, and they could take it all in with one mental glance. However it is expressed, all seem in agreement that the experience was over in an instant of earthly time.

Yet, despite its rapidity, my informants agree that the review, almost always described as a display of visual imagery, is incredibly vivid and real. In some cases, the images are reported to be in vibrant color, three-dimensional, and even moving. And even if they are flickering rapidly by, each image is perceived and recognized. Even the emotions and feelings associated with the images may be re-experienced as one is viewing them.

Some of those I interviewed claim that, while they cannot adequately explain it, everything they had ever done was there in this review—from the most insignificant to the most meaningful. Others explain that what they saw were mainly the highlights of their lives. Some have stated to me that even for a period of time following their experience of the review they could recall the events of their lives in incredible detail.

Some people characterize this as an educational effort on the part of the being of light. As they witness the display, the being seems to stress the importance of two things in life: Learning to love other people and acquiring knowledge. Let us look at a representative account of this type.

When the light appeared, the first thing he said to me was "What do you have to show me that you've done with your life?", or something to this effect. And that's when these flashbacks started. I thought, "Gee, what is going on?", because, all of a sudden, I was back early in my childhood. And from then on, it was like I was walking from the time of my very early life, on through each year of my life, right up to the present.

It was really strange where it started, too, when I was a little girl, playing down by the creek in our neighborhood, and there were other scenes from about that time—experiences I had had with my sister, and things about neighborhood people, and actual places I had been. And then I was in kindergarten, and I remembered the time when I had this one toy I really liked, and I broke it and I cried for a long time. This was a really traumatic experience for me. The images continued on through my life and I remembered when I was in Girl Scouts and went camping, and remembered many things about all the years of grammar school. Then, when I was in junior high school, it was a real big honor to be chosen for the scholastic achievement society, and I remembered when I was chosen. So, I went on through junior high, and then senior high school, and graduation, and up through my first few years of college, up to where I was then.

The things that flashed back came in the order of my life, and they were so vivid. The scenes were just like you walked outside and saw them, completely three-dimensional, and in color. And they moved. For instance, when I saw myself breaking the toy, I could see all the movements. It wasn't like I was watching it all from my perspective at the time. It was like the little girl I saw was somebody else, in a movie, one little girl among all the other children out there playing on the playground. Yet, it was me. I saw myself doing these things, as a child, and they were the exact same things I had done, because I remember them.

Now, I didn't actually see the light as I was going through the flashbacks. He disappeared as soon as he asked me what I had done, and the flashbacks started, and yet I knew that he was there with me the whole time, that he carried me back through the flashbacks, because I felt his presence, and because he made comments here and there. He was trying to show me something in each one of these flashbacks. It's not like he was trying to see what I had done—he knew already—but he was picking out these certain flashbacks of my life and putting them in front of me so that I would have to recall them.

All through this, he kept stressing the importance of love. The places where he showed it best involved my sister; I have always been very close to her. He showed me some instances where I had been selfish to my sister, but then just as many times where I had really shown love to her and had shared with her. He pointed out to me that I should try to do things for other people, to try my best. There wasn't any accusation in any of this, though. When he came across times when I had been selfish, his attitude was only that I had been learning from them, too.

He seemed very interested in things concerning knowledge, too. He kept on pointing out things that had to do with learning, and he did say that I was going to continue learning, and he said that even when he comes back for me (be-

cause by this time he had told me that I was going back) that there will always be a quest for
knowledge. He said that it is a continuous process, so I got the feeling that it goes on after
death. I think that he was trying to teach me, as
we went through those flashbacks.

The whole thing was really odd. I was there; I
was actually seeing these flashbacks; I was actually
walking through them, and it was so fast. Yet, it
was slow enough that I could take it all in. Still,
the time span wasn't all that large, I don't believe. It just seemed that the light came, and then
I went through these flashbacks, and the light
came back. It seems that it was less than five
minutes, and probably more than thirty seconds,
but I can't really tell you.

The only time I felt scared was when I was
concerned that I wasn't going to be able to finish
my life here. But I enjoyed going through this
flashback. That was fun. I had a good time going
back to my childhood, almost like I was reliving
it. It was a way of going back and seeing it which
you ordinarily just can't do.

It must also be pointed out that reports exist in
which the review is experienced even though the
being of light does not appear. As a rule, in experiences in which the being does apparently "direct" it, the review is a more overwhelming experience. Nonetheless, it is usually characterized
as quite vivid and rapid, and as accurate, regardless of whether or not the being of light appears,
and regardless of whether it occurs in the course of
an actual "death" or only during a close brush with
death.

After all this banging and going through this long, dark place, all of my childhood thoughts, my whole entire life was there at the end of this tunnel, just flashing in front of me. It was not exactly in terms of pictures, more in the form of thought, I guess. I can't exactly describe it to you, but it was just all there. It was just all there at once, I mean, not one thing at a time, blinking off and on, but it was everything, everything at one time. I thought about my mother, about things that I had done wrong. After I could see the mean little things I did as a child, and thought about my mother and father, I wished that I hadn't done these things, and I wished I could go back and undo them.

In the following two instances, although no clinical death had occurred at the time of the experience, actual physiological stress or injury was taking place.

The whole situation developed very suddenly. I had had a slight fever and had not felt well for about two weeks, but this night I rapidly became very ill and I felt much worse. I was lying in bed, and I remember trying to reach over to my wife and say that I was very sick, but I found it impossible to move. Beyond that, I found myself in a completely black void, and my whole life kind of flashed in front of me. It started back when I was six or seven years old, and I remembered a good friend I had in grammar school. I went from grammar school to high school to college, then to dental school, and then right on into practicing dentistry.

I knew I was dying, and I remember thinking

that I wanted to provide for my family. I was distraught that I was dying and yet that there were certain things that I had done in my life that I regretted, and other things that I regretted that I had left undone.

This flashback was in the form of mental pictures, I would say, but they were much more vivid than normal ones. I saw only the high points, but it was so rapid it was like looking through a volume of my entire life and being able to do it within seconds. It just flashed before me like a motion picture that goes tremendously fast, yet I was fully able to see it, and able to comprehend it. Still, the emotions didn't come back with the pictures, because there wasn't enough time.

I didn't see anything else during this experience. There was just blackness, except for the images I saw. Yet, I definitely felt the presence of a very powerful, completely loving being there with me all through this experience.

It is really interesting. When I recovered, I could tell everyone about every part of my life, in great detail, because of what I had been through. It's quite an experience, but it's difficult to put into words, because it happens so rapidly, yet it's so clear.

A young veteran describes his review:

While I was serving in Viet Nam, I received wounds, and I later "died" from them, yet through it all I knew exactly what was going on. I was hit with six rounds of machine gun fire, and as it happened I wasn't upset at all. In my mind, I actually felt relieved when I was wounded. I felt completely at ease, and it was not frightening.

At the point of impact, my life began to become a picture in front of me, and it seemed that I could go back to the time when I was still a baby, and the pictures seemed to progress through my whole life.

I could remember everything; everything was so vivid. It was so clear in front of me. It shot right by me from the earliest things I can remember right on up to the present, and it all happened within a short time. And it was not anything bad at all; I went through it with no regrets, no derogatory feelings about myself at all.

The best thing I can think of to compare it to is a series of pictures; like slides. It was just like someone was clicking off slides in front of me, very quickly.

Finally, here is a case of an extreme emotional emergency, in which death was imminent, although no actual injuries took place.

The summer after my first year in college, I took a job driving a large semi-tractor-trailer truck. I had a problem that summer with falling asleep behind the wheel. Early one morning I was driving the truck on a long trip, and I was nodding. The last thing I remember was seeing a road sign, and then I dozed off, and the next thing I knew, I heard an awful scraping and the right outside tire blew out, and then because of the weight and sway of the truck the left tires blew out, and the truck turned over on its side and went skidding down the road towards a bridge. I was scared because I knew what was happening. I knew the truck was going to hit the bridge.

Now, during the period of time that the truck was skidding, I just thought of all the things that I had done. I only saw certain things, the high points, and it was such a real thing. The first thing I remembered was following my father as he walked along the beach; it was when I was two years old. And there were a few other things, in order, from my early years, and after that I remembered breaking my new red wagon I had gotten for Christmas when I was five. I remember crying as I went to school in the first grade, wearing that gaudy yellow raincoat my mother had bought me. I remembered a little something about each one of my years in grammar school. I remember each of my teachers, and a little something that stood out about each year. Then I went to junior high, and got a paper route, and went to work in a grocery store, and it brought me up to right then, just before beginning my second year in college.

All these things, and many others, just flashed across my mind, and it was very quick. It probably didn't last but a split second. And then it was all over and I was standing there looking at the truck, and I thought I was dead, I thought I was an angel. I started pinching myself to see if I was alive, or a ghost, or what.

The truck was a total wreck, but I didn't receive a scratch. Somehow, I had jumped out the front windshield, because all the glass was blown out. After things calmed down, I thought it was strange that these things that had happened in my life, that had made some sort of lasting impression on me, had gone through my mind during this moment of crisis. I could probably think of all those things and remember and picture each of them now, but it would probably take me at least fifteen minutes. Yet, this had all come at once, automatically, and in less than a second. It was amazing.

The Border Or Limit

In a few instances, persons have described to me how during their near-death experience they seemed to be approaching what might be called a border or a limit of some kind. This has taken the form, in various accounts, of a body of water, a gray mist, a door, a fence across a field, or simply a line. Though this is highly speculative, one could raise the question of whether there might not be some one basic experience or idea at the root of all of them. If this is true, then the different versions would merely represent varying individual ways of interpreting, wording, or remembering the root experience. Let us look at a few accounts in which the idea of a border or limit plays a prominent role.

(1) I "died" from a cardiac arrest, and, as I did, I suddenly found myself in a rolling field. It was beautiful, and everything was an intense green —a color unlike anything on earth. There was light—beautiful, uplifting light—all around me. I looked ahead of me, across the field, and I saw a fence. I started moving towards the fence, and I saw a man on the other side of it, moving

towards it as if to meet me. I wanted to reach him, but I felt myself being drawn back, irresistibly. As I did, I saw him, too, turn around and go back in the other direction, away from the fence.

(2) This experience took place during the birth of my first child. About the eighth month of my pregnancy, I developed what my doctor described as a toxic condition and advised me to enter the hospital where he could force labor. It was immediately after delivery that I had a severe hemorrhage and the doctor had a difficult time controlling it. I was aware of what was happening as, having been a nurse myself, I realized the danger. At this time, I lost consciousness, and heard an annoying buzzing, ringing sound. The next thing I knew it seemed as if I were on a ship or a small vessel sailing to the other side of a large body of water. On the distant shore, I could see all of my loved ones who had died— my mother, my father, my sister, and others. I could see them, could see their faces, just as they were when I knew them on earth. They seemed to be beckoning me to come on over, and all the while I was saying, "No, no, I'm not ready to join you. I don't want to die. I'm not ready to go."

Now, this was the strangest experience because all this time I could see all the doctors and nurses, too, as they worked on my body, but it seemed as if I were a spectator rather than that person—that body—they were working on. I was trying so hard to get through to my doctor, "I'm not going to die," but no one could hear me. Everything—the doctors, the nurses, the delivery room, the ship, the water, and the far shore— was just sort of a conglomerate. It was all together, as if one scene were superimposed right on top of the other.

Finally, the ship almost reached the far shore, but just before it did, it turned around and started back. I did finally get through to my doctor, and I was saying, "I'm not going to die." It was at this point, I guess, that I came around, and the doctor explained what had happened, that I had had a post-partum hemorrhage, and that they had nearly lost me, but that I was going to be all right.

(3) I was hospitalized for a severe kidney condition, and I was in a coma for approximately a week. My doctors were extremely uncertain as to whether I would live. During this period when I was unconscious, I felt as though I were lifted right up, just as though I didn't have a physical body at all. A brilliant white light appeared to me. The light was so bright that I could not see through it, but going into its presence was so calming and so wonderful. There is just no experience on earth like it. In the presence of the light, the thoughts or words came into my mind: "Do you want to die?" And I replied that I didn't know since I knew nothing about death. Then the white light said, "Come over this line and you will learn." I felt that I knew where the line was in front of me, although I could not actually see it. As I went across the line, the most wonderful feelings came over me—feelings of peace, tranquility, a vanishing of all worries.

(4) I had a heart attack, and I found myself in a black void, and I knew I had left my physical body behind. I knew I was dying, and I thought, "God, I did the best I knew how at the time I did

it. Please help me." Immediately, I was moved out of that blackness, through a pale gray, and I just went on, gliding and moving swiftly, and in front of me, in the distance, I could see a gray mist, and I was rushing toward it. It seemed that I just couldn't get to it fast enough to satisfy me, and as I got closer to it I could see through it. Beyond the mist, I could see people, and their forms were just like they are on the earth, and I could also see something which one could take to be buildings. The whole thing was permeated with the most gorgeous light—a living, golden yellow glow, a pale color, not like the harsh gold color we know on earth.

As I approached more closely, I felt certain that I was going through that mist. It was such a wonderful, joyous feeling; there are just no words in human language to describe it. Yet, it wasn't my time to go through the mist, because instantly from the other side appeared my Uncle Carl, who had died many years earlier. He blocked my path, saying, "Go back. Your work on earth has not been completed. Go back now." I didn't want to go back, but I had no choice, and immediately I was back in my body. I felt that horrible pain in my chest, and I heard my little boy crying, "God, bring my mommy back to me."

(5) I was taken to the hospital for a critical condition they said was an "inflammation" and my doctor said I wasn't going to make it. He told my relatives to come because I wasn't going to be here much longer. They came, and gathered around my bed, and as the doctor thought I was dying, my relatives looked like they were going farther away from me. It looked like they

were going back instead of me going away from them. It got dimmer and dimmer, but I saw them. I lost consciousness and didn't seem to know anything else about what was going on in the hospital room, but I was in a narrow, v-shaped passage, like a trough, about the width of this chair. It just fit my body, and my hands and arms seemed to be down at my side. I went head first, and it was dark, dark as it could be in there. I moved on through it, downward, and I looked up and saw a beautiful, polished door, with no knob. Around the edges of the door I could see a really brilliant light, with rays just streaming like everybody was so happy in there, and reeling around, moving around. It seemed like it was awfully busy in there. I looked up and said, "Lord, here I am. If you want me, take me." Boy, he shot me back so fast it felt like I almost lost my breath.

Coming Back

Obviously, all the persons with whom I have talked had to "come back" at some point in their experience. Usually, though, an interesting change in their attitude had taken place by this time. Remember that the most common feelings reported in the first few moments following death are a desperate desire to get back into the body and an intense regret over one's demise. However, once the dying person reaches a certain depth in his experience, he does not want to come back, and he may even resist the return to the body. This is especially the case for those who have gotten so far as to encounter the being of light. As one man put it, most emphatically, "I *never* wanted to leave the presence of this being."

Exceptions to this generalization are often only apparent, not real. Several women who were mothers of young children at the time of their experience have told me that, while for *themselves* they would have preferred to stay where they were, they felt an obligation to try to go back and to raise their children.

I wondered whether I should stay there, but as I did I remembered my family, my three children and my husband. Now, this is the part that is hard to get across: When I had this wonderful feeling, there in the presence of that light, I really didn't want to come back. But I take my responsibilities very seriously, and I knew that I had a duty to my family. So I decided to try to come back.

In several other cases, persons have told me that, though they were comfortable and secure in their new disembodied existence and were even enjoying it, they felt happy to be able to return to physical life since they had left some important task undone. In a few cases, this has taken the form of a desire to complete an unfinished education.

I had completed three years of college and had only one more year to go. I kept thinking, "I don't want to die now." But I feel that if this had gone on just a few minutes more, if I had been with this light for just a little while longer, I wouldn't have thought of my education anymore, that I would've been taken up with the other things I was experiencing.

The accounts I have collected present an extremely varied picture when it comes to the question of the mode of return to physical life and of why the return took place. Most say simply that they do not know how or why they returned, or that they can only make guesses. A few very definitely feel that their own decisions to get back to the body and to return to earthly life were the operative factors.

I was out of my body, and I realized that I had to make a decision. I knew that I could not stay out of my physical body for a very long period of time so—well, for others this is very hard to understand, but for me then it was perfectly clear— I knew that I had to decide whether to move on out or to get back in.

It was wonderful over there on the other side, and I kind of wanted to stay. But knowing that I had something good to do on earth was just as wonderful in a way. So, I was thinking, "Yes, I must go back and live," and I got back into my physical body. I almost feel as though I stopped the bleeding myself. At any rate, I began to recover after that.

Others feel that they were in effect *allowed* to live by "God," or by the being of light, either in response to their own request to be allowed to live (usually because the request was made unselfishly) or because God or the being apparently had some mission in mind for them to fulfill.

I was above the table, and I could see everything they were doing. I knew that I was dying, that this would be it. Yet, I was concerned about my children, about who would take care of them. So, I was not ready to go. The Lord permitted me to live.

As one man remembers,

I say God surely was good to me, because I was dead, and he let the doctors bring me back, for a purpose. The purpose was to help my wife, I think, because she had a drinking problem, and I know that she just couldn't have made it without me. She is better now, though, and I really think it had a lot to do with what I went through.

A young mother feels that,

The Lord sent me back, but I don't know why. I definitely felt Him there, and knew that He recognized me and knew who I was. And yet He didn't see fit to let me into heaven; but why, I don't know. I have thought about it many times since, and I believe that it was either because I had those two small children to raise, or because I personally just wasn't ready to be there. I am still seeking the answer, and I just can't figure it out.

In a few instances, persons have expressed the feeling that the love or prayers of others have in effect pulled them back from death regardless of their own wishes.

I was with my elderly aunt during her last illness, which was very drawn out. I helped take care of her, and all that time everyone in the family was praying for her to regain her health. She stopped breathing several times, but they brought her back. Finally, one day she looked at me and she said, "Joan, I have been over there, over to the beyond and it is beautiful over there. I want to stay, but I can't as long as you keep praying for me to stay with you. Your prayers are holding me over here. Please don't pray any more." We did all stop, and shortly after that she died.

A woman told me,

The doctor had already said that I was gone, but I lived through it. Yet, the experience I had been through was so joyous, I had no bad feelings at all. As I came back, I opened my eyes, and my sister and my husband saw me. I could see their relief, and tears were pouring from their eyes. I could see that it was a relief to them that I did survive. I felt as though I had been called back—magnetized back—through the love of my sister and my husband. Since then, I have believed that other people can draw you back.

In quite a few instances, persons recall being drawn rapidly back through the dark tunnel through which they went during the initial moments of their experience. One man who died, for example, relates how he was propelled forward through a dark valley. He felt he was approaching the end of the tunnel, yet just at that moment he heard his name called from behind. He then was drawn backwards through the same space.

Few experience the actual re-entry into their physical bodies. Most report that they simply felt that at the end of their experience they "went to sleep" or lapsed into unconsciousness, later to awaken in their physical bodies.

> I don't remember getting back into my body. It was like I just drifted away, went to sleep, and then all of a sudden I woke right back up and I was lying in the bed. The people in the room were, in comparison, where they had been while I had been out of my body, looking at it and at them.

On the other hand, some remember being drawn speedily back towards their physical bodies, often with a jerk, at the end of their experiences.

> I was up there at the ceiling, watching them work on me. When they put the shocks on my chest, and my body jumped up, I just fell right back down to my body, just like dead weight. The next thing I knew, I was in my body again.

And

And I decided that I would come back, and when I did, it was like a jolt, like a jolt back into my body, and I felt that at that very moment I crossed back over into life.

In the very few accounts in which the event is recalled in some detail, re-entry is said to occur "through the head."

My "being" seemed to have a small end and a large end, and at the end of my accident, after it had just hung suspended over my head, it came back in. When it left my body, it seemed that the large end left first, but coming back in, the small end seemed to come in first.

One person recounted:

When I saw them pick up my body and take it out from under the steering wheel, it was just like a swooooosh and I felt like I was drawn through a limited area, a kind of funnel, I guess. It was dark and black in there, and I moved through it quickly, back to my body. And as I was being sucked back, it seemed that the suction started from the head, like I went into the head. I didn't feel that I had any say-so about it at all, nor even any time to think about it. I was there, yards away from my body, and all of a sudden, it was over with. I didn't even have time to think, "I'm being sucked back into my body."

Typically, the moods and feelings which were associated with the experience linger on for some time after the actual medical crisis has been resolved.

(1) After I came back, I cried off and on for about a week because I had to live in this world after seeing that one. I didn't want to come back.

(2) When I came back, I brought with me some of the wonderful feelings I had over there. They lasted for several days. Even now I feel them sometimes.

(3) This feeling was so indescribable. It has stayed with me, in a way. I've never forgotten it. I still think about it very often.

Telling Others

It must be emphasized that a person who has been through an experience of this type has no doubt whatsoever as to its reality and its importance. Interviews which I have done are usually sprinkled with remarks to precisely that effect. For example:

While I was out of my body, I was really amazed at what was happening to me. I couldn't understand it. But it was real. I saw my body so plainly, and from so far away. My mind wasn't at that point where I wanted to make things happen or make up anything. My mind wasn't manufacturing ideas. I just wasn't in that state of mind.

And

It was nothing like an hallucination. I have had hallucinations once, when I was given codeine in the hospital. But that had happened long before the accident which really killed me. And this experience was nothing like the hallucinations, nothing like them at all.

Such remarks come from persons who are very capable of distinguishing dream and fantasy from reality. The people I have interviewed are functional, well-balanced personalities. Yet, they do not tell their experiences as they would dreams, but rather as real events which actually happened to them.

Despite their own certainty of the reality and importance of what has happened to them, they realize that our contemporary society is just not the sort of environment in which reports of this nature would be received with sympathy and understanding. Indeed, many have remarked that they realized from the very beginning that others would think they were mentally unstable if they were to relate their experiences. So, they have resolved to remain silent on the subject or else to reveal their experiences only to some very close relative.

It was very interesting. It's just that I don't like telling people about it. People just kind of look at you like you're crazy.

Another recalls,

I didn't tell anyone about it for a long, long time. I just didn't say anything at all about it. I felt funny about it because I was afraid that nobody would think I was telling the truth, that they would say, "Oh, you're making up these things."

One day, I decided, "Well, I'll see how my family reacts to it," and I told them, but never anyone else until now. But I think that my family realized that I had been that far.

Others tried at first to tell someone else, but were rebuffed, so they resolved from then on to remain silent.

(1) The only person I tried to tell was my mother. Just a little later I mentioned to her how I had felt. But I was just a little boy, and she didn't pay any attention to me. So I never told it to anybody else.

(2) I tried to tell my minister, but he told me I had been hallucinating, so I shut up.

(3) I was pretty popular in junior high and high school, and I just floated with the crowd, never anything new. I was a follower, not a leader. And after this happened to me, and I tried to tell people, they just automatically labeled me as crazy, I think. I would try to tell people this, and they would listen with interest, but then I would find out later that they'd go say, "She has really flipped out." When I saw that it was just a big joke, I quit trying to communicate about it. I hadn't been trying to get across the idea that, "Gee, this strange experience has happened to me." What I was trying to say was that there was more we needed to know about life than I had ever thought about, and I am sure they hadn't, either.

(4) I tried to tell my nurses what had happened when I woke up, but they told me not to talk about it, that I was just imagining things.

So, in the words of one person,

You learn very quickly that people don't take to this as easily as you would like for them to. You simply don't jump up on a little soapbox and go around telling everyone these things.

Interestingly enough, in only one of the cases I have studied did a physician reveal any familiarity at all with near-death experiences or express any sympathy with them. After her out-of-body experience, one girl told me,

My family and I asked the doctor about what had happened to me, and he said that this happened a lot when a person is in severe pain or has severe injuries, that their soul will leave their body.

Considering the skepticism and lack of understanding that greet the attempt of a person to discuss his near-death experience, it is not surprising that almost everyone in this situation comes to feel that he is unique, that no one else has ever undergone what he has. For example, one man told me, "I have been somewhere nobody else has ever been."

It has often happened that when, after first interviewing someone in detail about his own experience, I have proceeded to tell him that others have reported exactly the same events and perceptions, he has expressed profound feelings of relief.

> It is a very interesting thing to find out that other people have had the same experience, because I hadn't realized. . . . I am actually happy that I have heard this, knowing that obviously someone else has been through this, too. Now I *know* I'm not crazy.

> It was always such a real thing to me, but I never would tell anybody because I was scared that they would look at me and think, "When you arrested, your mind went bad at the same time!"

> I figured that someone else would've had this same experience, but that I probably never would meet up with anybody who knew another person who had, because I don't think people are going to talk. If somebody were to come up and tell me, without me ever having been there, I would probably look at them and wonder what they were trying to pull over on me, because that's just the way our society is.

There is yet another reason why some are reticent to relate their experiences to others. They feel that the experience is so indescribable, so far beyond human language and human modes of perception and existence, that it is fruitless even to try.

Effects On Lives

For the reasons just explained, no one in my experience has built himself a portable lectern and gone out to preach about his experience on a full-time basis. No one has seen fit to proselytize, to try to convince others of the realities he experienced. Indeed, I have found that the difficulty is quite the reverse: People are naturally very reticent to tell others about what happened to them.

The effects which their experiences have had on their lives seem to have taken subtler, quieter forms. Many have told me that they felt that their lives were broadened and deepened by their experience, that because of it they became more reflective and more concerned with ultimate philosophical issues.

At this time—it was before I had gone off to college—I had grown up in a very small town, with very small-minded people, the people I was associated with, anyway. I was a typical high-school fraternity brat. You just weren't "it" unless you belonged to my fraternity.

But after this thing happened to me, I wanted to know more. At the time, though, I didn't think there was a person who would know anything about this, because I had never been out of this little world that I was in. I didn't know anything about psychology, or anything like that. All I knew was that I felt like I had aged overnight after this happened, because it opened up a whole new world for me that I never knew could possibly exist. I kept thinking, "There's so much that I've got to find out." In other words, there's more to life than Friday night movies and the football game. And there's more to me that I don't even know about. And then I started thinking about "What is the limit of the human and of the mind?" It just opened me up to a whole new world.

Another states,

Since then, it has been on my mind constantly what I have done with my life, and what I will do with my life. My past life—I'm satisfied with it. I don't think the world owes me anything because I really did everything I wanted and I did it the way I wanted to, and I'm still alive and I can do some more. But since I died, all of a sudden, right after my experience, I started wondering whether I had been doing the things I had done because they were good, or because they were good for *me*. Before, I just reacted off the impulse, and now I run things through my mind first, nice and slow. Everything seems to have to go through my mind and be digested, first.

I try to do things that have more meaning, and that makes my mind and soul feel better. And I try not to be biased, and not to judge people. I want to do things because they are good, not because they are good to me. And it seems that the understanding I have of things now is so much better. I feel like this is because of what happened to me, because of the places I went and the things I saw in this experience.

Others report a changed attitude or approach towards the physical life to which they have returned. One woman, for instance, says quite simply that "it made life much more precious to me."

Another person relates how,

It was a blessing in a way, because before that heart attack I was too busy planning for my children's future, and worrying about yesterday, that I was losing the joys of the present. I have a much different attitude now.

A few have mentioned that what they underwent changed their concepts of the mind and of the relative importance of the physical body as against the mind. This is illustrated especially well in these words of a woman who had an out-of-body experience while near death.

I was more conscious of my mind at the time than of that physical body. The mind was the most important part, instead of the shape of the body. And before, all my life, it had been exactly reversed. The body was my main interest and what was going on in my mind, well, it was just going on, and that's all. But after this happened, my mind was the main point of attraction, and the body was second—it was only something to encase my mind. I didn't care if I had a body or not. It didn't matter because for all I cared my mind was what was important.

In a very small number of cases, persons have told me that after their experiences they seemed to acquire or to notice faculties of intuition bordering on the psychic.

(1) Following this experience, it almost seemed as if I were filled with a new spirit. Since then, many have remarked to me that I seem to have

almost a calming effect on them, instantly, when they are troubled. And it seems that I am more in tune with people now, that I can pick up things about them faster.

(2) One thing that I think has been given to me, because of my death experience, is that I can sense the needs in other individuals' lives. Often, for instance when I have been with people on the elevator in the office building where I work, it seems I can almost read their faces, and tell that they need help, and what kind. Many times, I have spoken to people who are troubled like this, and have led them into my office for counseling.

(3) Since I was hurt, I've had the feeling of picking up people's thoughts and vibrations, and I can feel resentment from other people. I have often been able to pick up what people were going to say before they said it. Not many people will believe me, but I've had some really odd, odd experiences since then. One time, I was at a party and was picking up other people's thoughts, and some people there who didn't know me got up and left. They were scared that I was a witch or something. I don't know if it is something I picked up while I was dead, or if it was there dormant and I never did use it until after this happened.

There is a remarkable agreement in the "lessons," as it were, which have been brought back from these close encounters with death. Almost everyone has stressed the importance in this life of trying to cultivate love for others, a love of a unique and profound kind. One man who met the being of light felt totally loved and accepted, even while his whole life was displayed in a panorama for the being to see. He felt that the "question" that the being was asking him was whether he was able to love others in the same way. He now feels that it is his commission while on earth to try to learn to be able to do so.

In addition, many others have emphasized the importance of seeking knowledge. During their experiences, it was intimated to them that the acquisition of knowledge continues even in the after-life. One woman, for example, has taken advantage of every educational opportunity she has had since her "death" experience. Another man offers the advice, "No matter how old you are, don't stop learning. For this is a process, I gather, that goes on for eternity."

No one that I interviewed has reported coming out of this experience feeling morally "purified" or perfected. No one with whom I have talked in any way evinces a "holier-than-thou" attitude. In fact, most have specifically brought up the point that they feel that they are still trying, still searching. Their vision left them with new goals, new moral principles, and a renewed determination to try to live in accordance with them, but with no feelings of instantaneous salvation or of moral infallibility.

New Views of Death

As one might reasonably expect, this experience has a profound effect upon one's attitude towards physical death, especially for those who had not previously expected that anything took place after death. In some form or another, almost every person has expressed to me the thought that he is no longer afraid of death. This requires clarification, though. In the first place, certain modes of death are obviously undesirable, and secondly, none of these persons are actively seeking death. They all feel that they have tasks to do as long as they are physically alive and would agree with the words of a man who told me, "I've got quite a lot of changing to do before I leave here." Likewise, all would disavow suicide as a means by which to return to the realms they glimpsed during their experiences. It is just that now the state of death itself is no longer forbidding to them. Let us look at some passages in which such attitudes are explained.

(1) I suppose this experience molded something in my life. I was only a child when it happened, only ten, but now, my entire life through, I am thoroughly convinced that there is life after death, without a shadow of a doubt, and I am not afraid to die. I am not. Some people I have known are so afraid, so scared. I always

smile to myself when I hear people doubt that there is an afterlife, or say, "When you're dead, you're gone." I think to myself, "They really don't know."

I've had many things happen to me in my life. In business, I've had a gun pulled on me and put to my temple. And it didn't frighten me very much, because I thought, "Well, if I really die, if they really kill me, I know I'll still live somewhere."

(2) When I was a little boy I used to dread dying. I used to wake up at night crying and having a fit. My mother and father would rush into the bedroom and ask what was wrong. I told them that I didn't want to die, but that I knew I had to, and asked if they could stop it. My mother would talk to me and tell me, "No, that's just the way it is and we all have to face it." She said that we all had to do it alone and that when the time came we would do it all right. And years later after my mother died I would talk about death with my wife. I still feared it. I didn't want it to come.

But since this experience, I don't fear death. Those feelings vanished. I don't feel bad at funerals anymore. I kind of rejoice at them, because I know what the dead person has been through.

I believe that the Lord may have sent this experience to me because of the way I felt about death. Of course, my parents comforted me, but the Lord *showed* me, whereas they couldn't do that. Now, I don't talk about all this, but I know, and I am perfectly satisfied.

(3) Now, I am not afraid to die. It's not that I have a death wish, or want to die right now. I

don't want to be living over there on the other side now, because I'm supposed to be living here. The reason why I'm not afraid to die, though, is that I know where I'm going when I leave here, because I've been there before.

(4) The last thing the light said to me, before I came back to my body, back to life, was—well, what it boiled down to was that he would be back. He was telling me that I was going to go on and live this time, but that there would be a time when he would be getting in touch with me again, and that I would actually die.

So I know that the light will come back, and the voice, but as to when, I'm not sure. I think that it'll be a very similar experience, but I think a better one, really, since now I know what to expect and won't be so confused. I don't think I want to go back anytime soon, though. I still want to do some things down here.

The reason why death is no longer frightening, as all of these excerpts express, is that after his experience a person no longer entertains any doubts about his survival of bodily death. It is no longer merely an abstract possibility to him, but a fact of his experience.

Remember that much earlier I discussed the "annihilation" concept, which uses "sleeping" and "forgetting" as its models of death. Persons who have "died" disavow models like this and choose analogies which portray death as a transition from one state to another, or as an entry into a higher state of consciousness or of being. One woman, whose deceased relatives were there to greet her at her death, compared death to a "homecoming." Others have likened it to other psychologically positive states, for example, to awakening, to graduating, and to escape from jail.

(1) Some say that we are not using the word "death" because we are trying to escape from it. That's not true in my case. After you've once had the experience that I had, you know in your heart that there's no such thing as death. You just graduate from one thing to another—like from grammar school to high school to college.

(2) Life is like imprisonment. In this state, we just can't understand what prisons these bodies are. Death is such a release—like an escape from prison. That's the best thing I can think of to compare it to.

Even those who previously had some traditional conviction about the nature of the afterlife world seem to have moved away from it to some degree following their own brushes with death. In fact, in all the reports I have gathered, not one person has painted the mythological picture of what lies hereafter. No one has described the cartoonist's heaven of pearly gates, golden streets, and winged, harp-playing angels, nor a hell of flames and demons with pitchforks.

So, in most cases, the reward-punishment model of the afterlife is abandoned and disavowed, even by many who had been accustomed to thinking in those terms. They found, much to their amazement, that even when their most apparently awful and sinful deeds were made manifest before the being of light, the being responded not with anger and rage, but rather only with understanding, and even with humor. As one woman went through the review of her life with this being, she saw some scenes in which she had failed to show love and had shown selfishness. Yet, she says, "His attitude when we came to these scenes was just that I had been learning, even then." In place of this old model, many seemed to have returned with a new model and a new understanding of the world beyond—a vision which features not unilateral judgement, but rather cooperative development towards the ultimate end of self-realization. According to these new views, development of the soul, especially in the spiritual faculties of love and knowledge, does not stop upon death. Rather, it continues on the other side, perhaps eternally, but certainly for a period of time and to a depth which can only be glimpsed, while we are still in physical bodies, "through a glass, darkly."

Corroboration

The question naturally arises whether any evidence of the reality of near-death experiences might be acquired independently of the descriptions of the experiences themselves. Many persons report being out of their bodies for extended periods and witnessing many events in the physical world during the interlude. Can any of these reports be checked out with other witnesses who were known to be present, or with later confirming events, and thus be corroborated?

In quite a few instances, the somewhat surprising answer to this question is, "yes." Furthermore, the description of events witnessed while out of the body tend to check out fairly well. Several doctors have told me, for example, that they are utterly baffled about how patients with no medical knowledge could describe in such detail and so correctly the procedure used in resuscitation attempts, even though these events took place while the doctors knew the patients involved to be "dead."

In several cases, persons have related to me how they amazed their doctors or others with reports of events they had witnessed while out of the body. While she was dying, for example, one girl went out of her body and into another room in the hospital where she found her older sister crying and saying, "Oh, Kathy, please don't die, please don't die." The older sister was quite baffled when, later, Kathy told her exactly where she had been and what she had been saying, during this time. In the two passages which follow, similar events are described.

(1) After it was all over, the doctor told me that I had a really bad time, and I said, "Yeah, I know." He said, "Well, how do you know?" and I said, "I can tell you everything that happened."

He didn't believe me, so I told him the whole story, from the time I stopped breathing until the time I was kind of coming around. He was really shocked to know that I knew everything that had happened. He didn't know quite what to say, but he came in several times to ask me different things about it.

(2) When I woke up after the accident, my father was there, and I didn't even want to know what sort of shape I was in, or how I was, or how the doctors thought I would be. All I wanted to talk about was the experience I had been through. I told my father who had dragged my body out of the building, and even what color clothes that person had on, and how they got me out, and even about all the conversation that had been going on in the area. And my father said, "Well, yes, these things were true." Yet, my body was physically out this whole time, and there was no way I could have seen or heard these things without being outside of my body.

Finally, in a few cases, I have been able to get the independent testimony of others about corroborating events. In assessing the evidential value of such independent reports, however, several complicating factors arise. First, in most of the cases the corroborating event itself is attested to only by the dying person himself and by at most a couple of close friends and acquaintances. Second, even in the exceptionally dramatic, well-attested instances I have collected, I have promised not to reveal actual names. Even if I could, though, I do not think that such corroborating stories collected after the fact would constitute *proof*, for reasons which I shall explain in the final chapter.

We have reached the end of our survey of the various commonly-reported stages and events of the experience of dying. In closing this chapter, I want to quote at some length from a rather exceptional account which embodies many of the elements I have discussed. In addition, however, it contains a unique twist not encountered before: The being of light tells the man involved of his impending death in advance, and then decides subsequently to let him live.

At the time this happened I suffered, as I still do, with a very severe case of bronchial asthma and emphysema. One day, I got into a coughing fit and apparently ruptured a disk in the lower part of my spine. For a couple of months, I consulted a number of doctors for the agonizing pain, and finally one of them referred me to a neurosurgeon, Dr. Wyatt. He saw me and told me that I needed to be admitted to the hospital immediately, so I went on in and they put me in traction right away.

Dr. Wyatt knew that I had bad respiratory diseases so he called in a lung specialist, who said that the anesthesiologist, Dr. Coleman, should be consulted if I was going to be put to sleep. So the lung specialist worked on me for almost three weeks until he finally got me to a place where Dr. Coleman would put me under. He finally consented on a Monday, although he was very much worried about it. They scheduled the operation for the next Friday. Monday night, I went to sleep and had a restful sleep until sometime early Tuesday morning, when I woke up in severe pain. I turned over and tried to get in a more comfortable position, but just at that moment a light appeared in the corner of the room, just below the ceiling. It was just a ball of light, almost like a globe, and it was not very large, I would say no more than twelve to fifteen inches in diameter, and as this light appeared, a feeling came over me. I can't say that it was an eerie feeling, because it was not. It was a feeling of complete peace and utter relaxation. I could see a hand reach down for me from the light, and the light said, "Come with me. I want to show you something." So immediately, without any hesitation whatsoever, I reached up with my hand and grabbed onto the hand I saw. As I did, I had the feeling of being drawn up and of leaving my body, and I looked back and saw it lying there on the bed while I was going up towards the ceiling of the room.

Now, at this time, as soon as I left my body, I took on the same form as the light. I got the feeling, and I'll have to use my own words for it, because I've never heard anyone talk about anything like this, that this form was definitely a spirit. It wasn't a body, just a wisp of smoke or a vapor. It looked almost like the clouds of cigarette smoke you can see when they are illuminated as they drift around a lamp. The form I took had colors, though. There was orange, yellow, and a color that was very indistinct to me—I took it to be an indigo, a bluish color.

This spiritual form didn't have a shape like a body. It was more or less circular, but it had what I would call a hand. I know this because when the light reached down for me, I reached up for it with my hand. Yet, the arm and hand of my body just stayed put, because I could see them lying on the bed, down by the side of my body, as I rose up to the light. But when I wasn't using this spiritual hand, the spirit went back to the circular pattern.

So, I was drawn up to the same position the light was in, and we started moving through the ceiling and the wall of the hospital room, into the corridor, and through the corridor, down through the floors it seemed, on down to a lower floor in the hospital. We had no difficulty in passing through doors or walls. They would just fade away from us as we would approach them.

During this period it seemed that we were traveling. I knew we were moving, yet there was no sensation of speed. And in a moment, almost instantaneously, really, I realized that we had reached the recovery room of the hospital. Now, I hadn't even known where the recovery room was at this hospital, but we got there, and again, we were in the corner of the room near the ceiling, up above everything else. I saw the doctors and nurses walking around in their green suits and saw the beds that were placed around in there.

This being then told me—he showed me— "That's where you're going to be. When they bring you off the operating table they're going to put you in that bed, but you will never awaken from that position. You'll know nothing after you go to the operating room until I come back to get you sometime after this." Now, I won't say this was in words. It wasn't like an audible voice, because if it had been I would have expected the others in the room to have heard the voice, and they didn't. It was more of an impression that came to me. But it was in such a vivid form that there was no way for me to say I didn't hear it or I didn't feel it. It was definite to me.

And what I was seeing—well, it was so much easier to recognize things while I was in this spiritual form. I was now wondering, like, "Now, what is that that he is trying to show me." I knew immediately what it was, what he had in mind. There was no doubt. It was that *that bed*—it was the bed on the right just as you come in from the corridor—is where I'm going to be and he's brought me here for a purpose. And then he told me why. It came to me that the reason for this was that he didn't want any fear when the time came that my spirit passed from my body, but that he wanted me to know what the sensation would be on passing that point. He wanted to assure me so that I wouldn't be afraid, because he was telling me that he wouldn't be there immediately, that I would go through other things first, but that he would be overshadowing everything that happened and would be there for me at the end.

Now, immediately, when I had joined him to take the trip to the recovery room and had become a spirit myself, in a way we had been fused into one. We were two separate ones, too, of course. Yet, he had full control of everything that was going on as far as I was concerned. And even if we were traveling through the walls and ceilings and so forth, well, it just seemed that we were in such close communion that nothing whatsoever could have bothered me. Again, it was just a peacefulness, calmness, and a serenity that have never been found anywhere else.

So, after he told me this, he took me back to my

hospital room, and as I got back I saw my body again, still lying in the same position as when we left, and instantaneously I was back in my body. I would guess that I had been out of my body for five or ten minutes, but passage of time had nothing to do with this experience. In fact, I don't remember if I have ever even thought of it as being any particular time.

Now, this whole thing had just astounded me, took me completely by surprise. It was so vivid and real—more so than ordinary experience. And the next morning, I was not in the least afraid. When I shaved, I noticed that my hand didn't shake like it had been doing for six or eight weeks before then. I knew that I would be dying, and there was no regret, no fear. There was no thought, "What can I do to keep this from happening?" I was ready.

Now, on Thursday afternoon, the day before the operation the next morning, I was in my hospital room, and I was worried. My wife and I have a boy, an adopted nephew, and we were then having some trouble with him. So I decided to write a letter to my wife and one to my nephew, putting some of my worries in words, and to hide the letters where they wouldn't be found until after the operation. After I had written about two pages on the letter to my wife, it was just as if the floodgates had opened. All at once, I broke out in tears, sobbing. I felt a presence, and at first I thought maybe that I had cried so loud that I had disturbed one of the nurses, and that they had come in to see what was the matter with me. But I hadn't heard the door open. And again I felt this presence, but I didn't see any light this time, and thoughts or words came to me, just as before, and he said, "Jack, why are you crying? I thought you would be pleased to be with me." I thought, "Yes, I am. I want to go very much." And the voice said, "Then why are you crying?" I said, "We've had trouble with our nephew, you know, and I'm afraid my wife won't know how to raise him. I'm trying to put into words how I feel, and what I want her to try to do for him. I'm concerned, too, because I feel that maybe my presence could have settled him down some."

Then the thoughts came to me, from this presence, "Since you are asking for someone else, and thinking of others, not Jack, I will grant what you want. You will live until you see your nephew become a man." And just like that, it was gone. I stopped crying, and I destroyed the letter so my wife wouldn't accidentally find it.

That evening, Dr. Coleman came in and told me that he was expecting a lot of trouble with putting me to sleep, and for me not to be surprised to wake up and find a lot of wires and tubes and machines all around me. I didn't tell him what I had experienced, so I just nodded and said I would cooperate.

The next morning the operation took a long time but went fine, and as I was regaining my consciousness, Dr. Coleman was there with me, and I told him, "I know exactly where I am." He asked, "What bed are you in?" I said, "I'm in that first bed on the right just as you come in from the hall." He just kind of laughed, and of course, he thought that I was just talking from the anesthetic.

I wanted to tell him what had happened, but just in a moment Dr. Wyatt came in and said, "He's awake now. What do you want to do?" And

Dr. Coleman said, "There's not a thing I can do. I've never been so amazed in my life. Here I am with all this equipment set up and he doesn't need a thing." Dr. Wyatt said, "Miracles still happen, you know." So, when I could get up in the bed, and see around the room, I saw that I was in that same bed that the light had shown me several days before.

Now, all this was three years ago, but it is still just as vivid as it was then. It was the most fantastic thing that has ever happened to me, and it has made a big difference. But I don't talk about it. I have only told my wife, my brother, my minister, and now you. I don't know how to say it, but this is so hard to explain. I'm not trying to make a big explosion in your life, and I'm not trying to brag. It's just that after this, I don't have any doubts anymore. I know there is life after death.

3

PARALLELS

The events of the various stages of the experience of dying are, to say the very least, unusual. Hence, my surprise has been compounded as over the years I have come across quite a number of striking parallels to them. These parallels occur in ancient and/or highly esoteric writings from the literature of several very diverse civilizations, cultures, and eras.

The Bible

In our society *The Bible* is the most widely read and discussed book dealing with matters relating to the nature of the spiritual aspect of man and to life after death. On the whole, however, *The Bible* has relatively little to say about the events that transpire upon death, or about the precise nature of the after-death world. This is especially true of the *Old Testament*. According to some Biblical scholars, only two passages in all of the *Old Testament* speak unequivocally of life after death:

111

Isaiah 26:19: Thy dead men shall live, together with my dead body shall they arise. Awake and sing, ye that dwell in dust for . . . the earth shall cast out the dead.[1]

Daniel 12:2: And many of them that sleep in the dust of the earth shall awake, some to everlasting life, and some to shame and everlasting contempt.

Notice that in both of these passages there is the strong suggestion that a resurrection of the physical body will occur and that the state of physical death is compared here, again, to sleep.

Still, as is evident from the preceding chapter, a few persons have drawn upon specific Biblical concepts when trying to elucidate or to explain to me what happened to them. For instance, it will be remembered that one man identified the dark enclosure he went through at the moment of death as the Biblical "valley of the shadow of death." Two persons mentioned Jesus' claim, "I am the light of the world." Apparently, it was at least partly on the basis of that phrase that both identified the light they met as Christ. One of them told me, "I didn't ever see a person in this light, but to me the light was a Christ—consciousness, a oneness with all things, a perfect love. I think that Jesus meant it literally when he said he was the light of the world."

In addition, in my own reading I have come across a few seeming parallels which none of my subjects have mentioned. The most interesting ones occur in the writings of the apostle Paul. He was a persecutor of Christians until he had his famous vision and conversion on the road to Damascus. He says:

> Acts 26:13–26: At midday, O king, I saw in the way a light from heaven, above the brightness of the sun, shining round about me and them which journeyed with me. And when we were all fallen to the earth, I heard a voice speaking unto me, and saying in the Hebrew tongue, "Saul, Saul, why persecutest thou me? It is hard for thee to kick against the pricks."
>
> And I said, "Who art thou, Lord?" And he said, "I am Jesus, whom thou persecutest. But rise, and stand upon thy feet: for I have appeared unto thee for this purpose, to make thee a minister and a witness, both of these things which thou hast seen, and of those things in which I will appear unto thee. . . ."
>
> Whereupon, O King Agrippa, I was not disobedient unto the heavenly vision. . . . And as I thus spake for myself, Festus said with a loud voice, "Paul, thou art beside thyself; much learning doth make thee mad."
>
> But I said, "I am not mad, most noble Festus; but speak forth the words of truth and soberness."

This episode obviously bears some resemblance to the encounter with the being of light in near death experiences. First of all, the being is endowed with personality, though no physical form is seen, and a "voice" which asks a question and issues instructions emanates from it. When Paul tries to tell others, he is mocked and labeled as "insane." Nonetheless, the vision changed the course of his life: He henceforth became the leading proponent of Christianity as a way of life entailing love of others.

There are differences, too, of course. Paul did not come near death in the course of his vision. Also, interestingly enough, Paul reports that he was blinded by the light and was unable to see for three days afterward. This runs contrary to the reports of those who say that though the light was indescribably brilliant, it in no way blinded them, or kept them from seeing things around them.

In his discussions of the nature of the afterlife, Paul says that some challenge the Christian concept of the afterlife by asking what kind of body the dead will have:

1 Corinthians 15:35–52: But some man will say, "How are the dead raised up? And with what body do they come?" Thou fool. . . (of) that which thou sowest, thou sowest not that body that shall be, but bare grain. . . . But God giveth it a body as it hath pleased him, and to every seed his own body. . . . There are also celestial bodies, and bodies terrestrial: but the glory of the celestial is one and the glory of the terrestrial is another. . . . So also is the resurrection of the dead. It is sown in corruption, it is raised in incorruption: It is sown in dishonor; it is raised in glory: It is sown in weakness; it is raised in power: It is sown a natural body, it is raised a spiritual body. There is a natural body, and there is a spiritual body. . . . Behold I show you a mys-

tery: We shall not all sleep, but we shall all be changed. In a moment, in the twinkling of an eye, at the last trumpet: for the trumpet shall sound, and the dead shall be raised incorruptible.

Interestingly, Paul's brief sketch of the nature of the "spiritual body" corresponds very well with the accounts of those who have found themselves out of their bodies. In all cases, the immateriality of the spiritual body—its lack of physical substance—is stressed, as are its lack of limitations. Paul says, for example, that whereas the physical body was weak and ugly, the spiritual body will be strong and beautiful. This reminds one of the account of a near-death experience in which the spiritual body seemed whole and complete even when the physical body could be seen to be mutilated, and of another in which the spiritual body seemed to be of no particular age, *i.e.*, not limited by time.

Plato

The philosopher Plato, who was one of the greatest thinkers of all time, lived in Athens from 428 to 348 B.C. He left us a body of thought in the form of some twenty-two philosophical plays or dialogues, most of which include his teacher Socrates as chief interlocutor, and a small number of letters.

Plato believed strongly in the use of reason, logic, and argument in the attainment of truth and wisdom, but only up to a point, for in addition he was a great visionary who suggested that ultimately truth can only come to one in an almost mystical experience of enlightenment and insight. He accepted that there were planes and dimensions of reality other than the sensible, physical world and believed that the physical realm could be understood only by reference to these other, "higher" planes of reality. Accordingly, he was interested mainly in the incorporeal, conscious component of man—the soul—and saw the physical body only as the temporary vehicle of the soul. It is not surprising, then, that he was interested in the fate of the soul after physical death and that several of his dialogues—especially *Phaedo*, *Gorgias*, and *The Republic*—deal in part with that very topic.

Plato's writings are full of descriptions of death which are precisely like those which were discussed in the previous chapter. For instance, Plato defines death as the separation of the incorporeal part of a living person, the soul, from the physical part, the body. What is more, this incorporeal part of man is subject to many fewer limitations than is the physical part. Hence, Plato specifically points out that time is not an element of the realms beyond the physical, sensible world. The other realms are eternal, and, in Plato's striking phrase, what we call time is but the "moving, unreal reflection of eternity."

Plato discusses in various passages how the soul which has been separated from its body may meet and converse with the departed spirits of others and be guided through the transition from physical life to the next realm by guardian spirits. He mentions how some might expect to be met at the time of their death by a boat which takes them across a body of water to "the other shore" of their after-death existence. In *Phaedo* both the dramatic setting and the thrust of the arguments and words used drive home the point that the body is the prison of the soul and that, correspondingly, death is like an escape or release from that prison. While, as we saw in the first chapter, Plato articulates (through Socrates) the ancient view of death as a sleeping and a forgetting, he does so only ultimately to disavow it and, indeed, to turn it around 180°. According to Plato, the soul comes into the physical body from a higher and more divine realm of being. For him it is *birth* which is the sleeping and the forgetting, since the soul, in being born into the body, goes from a state of great awareness to a much less conscious one and in the meantime forgets the truths it knew while in its previous out-of-body state. Death, by implication, is an *awakening* and *remembering*. Plato remarks that the soul that has been separated from the body upon death can think and reason even more clearly than before, and that it can recognize things in their true nature far more readily. Furthermore, soon after

117

death it faces a "judgment" in which a divine being displays before the soul all the things—both good and bad—which it has done in its life and makes the soul face them.

In Book X of *The Republic* perhaps the most striking similarity of all occurs. There Plato recounts the myth of Er, a Greek soldier. Er went away to a battle in which many Greeks were killed, and when his countrymen went to collect the bodies of their war dead his body was among them. It was lain, along with all the others, upon a funeral pyre to be burned. After some time his body revived, and Er described what he had seen in his journey to the realms beyond. First of all, Er said, his soul went out of his body, he joined with a group of other spirits, and they went to a place where there were "openings" or "passageways" apparently leading from the earth into the realms of the afterlife. Here the other souls were stopped and judged by divine beings, who could see at a glance, in some sort of display, all the things that the soul had done while in its earthly life. Er, however, was not judged. Instead, the beings told him that he must go back to inform men in the physical world concerning what the other world was like. After seeing many other sights, Er was sent back, but he said that he was ignorant of how he was returned to his physical body. He merely woke up and found himself upon the funeral pyre.

It is important to bear in mind that Plato himself

warns us that he meant his descriptions of the precise details of the world the soul will enter after death to be "probabilities, at best." Though he does not doubt that survival of bodily death does occur, he insists that in trying to explain the afterlife while still in our present physical life we face two strong disadvantages. First of all, our souls are imprisoned in physical bodies and are thus limited in what they can experience and learn by our physical senses. Vision, hearing, touch, taste, and smell each in its own way may fool us. Our eyes may make an enormous object seem small if it is far away, we may mishear what someone says to us, and so on. All this may result in our having false opinions or impressions of the nature of things. So, our souls cannot see reality in itself until they are liberated from the distractions and inaccuracies of the physical senses.

Secondly, Plato says human language is inadequate to express the ultimate realities directly. Words conceal rather than reveal the inner natures of things. It follows that no human words can do more than indicate—by analogy, through myth, and in other indirect ways—the true character of that which lies beyond the physical realm.

The Tibetan Book of the Dead

This remarkable work was compiled from the teachings of sages over many centuries in prehistoric Tibet and passed down through these early generations by word of mouth. It was finally written down, apparently, in the eighth century, A.D., but even then was hidden to keep it secret from outsiders.

The form which this unusual book takes is shaped by the many interrelated uses to which it was put. First of all, the wise men who wrote it regarded dying as, in effect, a skill—something which could be done either artfully or in an unbecoming manner, depending upon whether one had the requisite knowledge to do it well. So, the book was read as part of the funeral ceremony, or to the dying person during the closing moments of his life. It thus was thought to serve two functions. The first was to help the dying person keep in mind the nature of each new wondrous phenomenon as he experienced it. The second was to help those still living think positive thoughts and not hold the dying one back with their love and emotional concern, so that he could enter into the afterdeath planes in a proper frame of mind, released from all bodily concerns.

To effect these ends, the book contains a lengthy description of the various stages through which the soul goes after physical death. The correspondence between the early stages of death which it relates and those which have been recounted to me by those who have come near to death is nothing short of fantastic.

First of all, in the Tibetan account the mind or

soul of the dying person departs from the body. At some time thereafter his soul enters a "swoon" and he finds himself in a void—not a physical void, but one which is, in effect, subject to its own kind of limits, and one in which his consciousness still exists. He may hear alarming and disturbing noises and sounds, described as roaring, thundering, and whistling noises, like the wind, and usually finds himself and his surroundings enveloped in a grey, misty illumination.

He is surprised to find himself out of his physical body. He sees and hears his relatives and friends mourning over his body and preparing it for the funeral and yet when he tries to respond to them they neither hear nor see him. He does not yet realize that he is dead, and he is confused. He asks himself whether he is dead or not, and, when he finally realizes that he is, wonders where he should go or what he should do. A great regret comes over him, and he is depressed about his state. For a while he remains near the places with which he has been familiar while in physical life.

He notices that he is still in a body—called the "shining" body—which does not appear to consist of material substance. Thus, he can go through rocks, walls, and even mountains without encountering any resistance. Travel is almost instantaneous. Wherever he wishes to be, he arrives there in only a moment. His thought and perception are less limited; his mind becomes very lucid and his senses seem more keen and more perfect and closer

121

in nature to the divine. If he has been in physical life blind or deaf or crippled, he is surprised to find that in his "shining" body all his senses, as well as all the powers of his physical body, have been restored and intensified. He may encounter other beings in the same kind of body, and may meet what is called a clear or pure light. The Tibetans counsel the dying one approaching this light to try to have only love and compassion towards others.

The book also describes the feelings of immense peace and contentment which the dying one experiences, and also a kind of "mirror" in which his entire life, all deeds both good and bad, are reflected for both him and the beings judging him to see vividly. In this situation, there can be no misrepresentation; lying about one's life is impossible.

In short, even though *The Tibetan Book of the Dead* includes many later stages of death which none of my subjects have gone so far as to experience, it is quite obvious that there is a striking similarity between the account in this ancient manuscript and the events which have been related to me by twentieth-century Americans.

Emanuel Swedenborg

Swedenborg, who lived from 1688 until 1772, was born in Stockholm. He was quite renowned in his day and made respectable contributions in various fields of natural science. His writings, at first oriented towards anatomy, physiology, and psychology, gained quite a bit of recognition. Later in his life, however, he underwent a religious crisis and began to tell of experiences in which he had purportedly been in communication with spiritual entities from beyond.

His later works abound with vivid descriptions of what life after death is like. Again, the correlation between what he writes of some of his spiritual experiences and what those who have come back from close calls with death report is amazing. For instance, Swedenborg describes how, when the bodily functions of respiration and circulation cease,

> Still man does not die, but is only separated from the corporeal part which was of use to him in the world. . . . Man, when he dies, only passes from one world into another.[2]

He claims that he himself has been through the early events of death, and has had experiences out of his body.

> I was brought into a state of insensibility as to the bodily senses, thus almost into the state of the dying; yet the interior life with thought remaining entire, so that I perceived and retained in memory the things which occurred, and which occur to those who are resuscitated from the dead. . . . Especially it was given to perceive . . .

that there was a drawing and . . . pulling of . . .
mind, thus of my spirit, from the body.

During this experience, he encounters beings
whom he identifies as "angels." They ask him, in
effect, if he is prepared to die.

Those angels first inquired what my thought
was, whether it was like the thought of those who
die, which is usually about eternal life; and that
they wished to keep my mind in that thought.

Yet, the communication which takes place between Swedenborg and the spirits is not of an
earthly, human kind. It is instead almost a direct
transfer of thoughts. Hence, there is no possibility
of misunderstanding.

Whereas spirits converse with each other by a
universal language. . . . Every man, immediately
after death, comes into this universal language
. . . which is proper to his spirit. . . .
The speech of an angel or a spirit with man is
heard as sonorously as the speech of a man with a
man; yet it is not heard by others who stand near,
but by himself alone; the reason is, because the
speech of an angel or spirit flows first into the
man's thought . . .

The newly dead person does not realize that he
is dead, for he is still in a "body" which resembles
his physical body in several respects.

The first state of man after death is similar to
his state in the world, because then in like manner

he is in externals. . . . Hence, he knows no otherwise than that he is still in the world. . . . Therefore, after they have wondered that they are in a body, and in every sense which they had in the world . . . they come into a desire of knowing what heaven is, and what hell is.

Yet, the spiritual state is less limited. Perception, thought, and memory are more perfect, and time and space no longer pose the obstacles they do in physical life.

All the faculties of spirits . . . are in a more perfect state, as well their sensations as their thoughts and perceptions.

The dying man may meet with other departed spirits whom he knew while in life. They are there to help him during his passage into the beyond.

The spirit of man recently departed from the world is . . . recognized by his friends, and by those whom he had known in the world . . . wherefore they are instructed by their friends concerning the state of eternal life. . . .

His past life may be shown to him in a vision. He remembers every detail of it, and there is no possibility of his lying or concealing anything.

The interior memory . . . is such that there are inscribed in it all the particular things . . . which man has at any time thought, spoken, and done . . . from his earliest infancy to extreme

125

old age. Man has with him the memory of all these things when he comes into another life, and is successively brought into all recollection of them. . . . All that he had spoken and done . . . are made manifest before the angels, in a light as clear as day . . . and . . . there is nothing so concealed in the world that it is not manifested after death . . . as if seen in effigy, when the spirit is viewed in the light of heaven.

Swedenborg describes too the "light of the Lord" which permeates the hereafter, a light of ineffable brightness which he has glimpsed himself. It is a light of truth and of understanding.

So again in the writings of Swedenborg, as before in *The Bible*, the works of Plato, and *The Tibetan Book of the Dead*, we find striking parallels to the events of contemporary near-death experiences. The question naturally arises, though, as to whether this parallelism is really all that surprising. Some might suggest, for instance, that the authors of these various works could have influenced one another. Such an assertion could be supported in some cases, but not in others. Plato admits that he derived some of his insights partly from the religious mysticism of the East, so he might have been influenced by the same tradition which produced *The Tibetan Book of the Dead*. The ideas of Greek philosophy, in turn, influenced certain *New Testament* writers, and so it could be argued that Paul's discussion of the spiritual body has some of its roots in Plato.

On the other hand, in most cases it is not easy to establish that such influence could have taken place. Each writer seems to bring up a few interesting details which also recur in my interviews, yet which he could not have gotten from earlier authors. Swedenborg read *The Bible* and was familiar with Plato. However, he several times alludes to the fact that someone who has just died may not realize that he is dead for some time. This fact, which comes out again and again in the narratives of those who have come very close to death, is apparently not mentioned either in *The Bible* or by Plato. Yet, it is emphasized in *The Tibetan Book of the Dead*, a work which Swedenborg could not possibly have read. Indeed, it was not even translated until 1927.

Is it possible that the near-death experiences I have collected were influenced by works of the kind which I have discussed? All of the persons with whom I have talked had some exposure prior to their experiences to *The Bible*, and two or three knew something about the ideas of Plato. On the other hand, none were aware of the existence of such esoterica as the works of Swedenborg or *The Tibetan Book of the Dead*. Yet, many details which do not appear in *The Bible*, or even in Plato, constantly crop up in the accounts which I have gathered, and these correspond exactly with phenomena and events mentioned in the more unusual sources.

It must be acknowledged that the existence of the similarities and parallels among the writings of ancient thinkers and the reports of modern Americans who survive close brushes with death remains a striking, and, so far, not definitively explicable fact. How is it, we might well ask ourselves, that the wisdom of Tibetan sages, the theology and visions of Paul, the strange insights and myths of Plato, and the spiritual revelations of Swedenborg all agree so well, both among themselves and with the narratives of contemporary individuals who have come as close as anyone alive to the state of death?

[1]All quotations from *The Bible* are taken from the King James Version.
[2]All Swedenborg quotations are taken from *Compendium of the Theological and Spiritual Writings of Emanuel Swedenborg* (Boston: Crosby and Nichols, 1853), pp. 160–197.

4
QUESTIONS

By now, many doubts and objections will have occurred to the reader. In the years that I have been giving talks, in private and in public, on this subject, I have been asked many questions. In general, I tend to be asked about the same things on most occasions, so I have been able to compile a list of those questions which are asked most frequently. In this chapter and the next I shall address myself to them.

Are you just making all this up?

No, I'm not. I very much want to pursue a career in the teaching of psychiatry and the philosophy of medicine, and attempting to perpetrate a hoax would hardly be conducive to that aim.

Also, it has been my experience that anyone who makes diligent and sympathetic inquiries among his own acquaintances, friends, and relatives about the occurrence of such experiences will soon have his doubts dispelled.

But aren't you being unrealistic? After all, how common are such experiences?

I am the first to admit that, due to the necessarily limited nature of my sample of cases, I am unable to give a statistically significant numerical estimate of the incidence or prevalence of this phenomenon. However, I am quite willing to say this: The occurrence of such experiences is far more common than anyone who hasn't studied them would guess. I have given many public lectures on this subject, to many kinds and sizes of groups, and there has never been an instance in which someone there didn't come up afterward with a story of his own, or even, in some cases, tell it publicly. Of course, one could always say (and truly!) that someone with such an experience would be more likely to come to a lecture on such a topic. Nonetheless, in many of the cases I have encountered, the person involved did not come to the lecture because of the topic. For example, I recently addressed a group of thirty persons. Two of them had had near-death experiences, and both were there just because they were members of the group. Neither knew the topic of my talk beforehand.

If near-death experiences are as common as you say, why isn't this fact more generally known?

There seem to be several reasons why this is so. First and foremost, I think, is the fact that the temper of our times is, in general, decidedly against discussion of the possibility of survival of bodily death. We live in an age in which science and technology have made enormous strides in understanding and conquering nature. To talk about life after death seems somehow atavistic to many who perhaps feel that the idea belongs more to our "superstitious" past than to our "scientific" present. Accordingly, persons who have experiences which lie outside the realm of science as we now understand it are ridiculed. Being aware of these attitudes, persons who have transcendent experiences are usually understandably reluctant to relate them very openly. I am convinced, in fact, that an enormous mass of material lies hidden in the minds of persons who have had such experiences but who, for fear of being labeled "crazy" or "over-imaginative," have never related them to more than one or two close friends or relatives.

In addition, the general public obscurity of the topic of near-death encounters seems to stem in part from a common psychological phenomenon involving attention. A lot of what we hear and see every day goes unregistered in our conscious minds. If our attention is drawn to something in a dramatic way, however, we tend to notice it thereafter. Many a person has had the experience of learning the meaning of a new word and then seeing the word in everything he picks up to read for the next few days. The explanation is usually not that the word has just taken hold in the language and is appearing everywhere. Rather, it is that the word has been there in the things he has been reading all along but that, not being aware of its meaning, he generally skipped over it without being consciously aware of it.

Similarly, after a lecture I recently gave I opened the floor for discussion and a doctor asking the first question said, "I have been in medicine for a long time. If these experiences are as common as you say they are, why haven't I heard of them?" Knowing that there would probably be someone there who had encountered a case or two, I immediately turned the question back to the audience. I asked, "Has anyone else here heard of anything like this?" At this point, the doctor's wife raised her hand and related the story of a very close friend of theirs.

To give another example, a physician I know first became aware of experiences of this kind by reading an old newspaper article about a speech I gave. The next day, a patient gave him, unsolicited, an account of a very similar experience. The physician established that the patient could not have heard of or read about my studies. Indeed, the patient confided his story only because he was baffled and somewhat alarmed by what had happened to him and was seeking a medical opinion. It may very well have been that in both instances, the doctors involved had heard of some cases of this before, but had thought of them as individual quirks rather than as a wide-spread phenomenon and had not fully paid attention to them.

Finally, there is an additional factor in the case of physicians which may help to account for why so many of them seem unaware of near-death phenomena, even though one would suspect that doctors, of all people, should have encountered them. In the course of their training, it is constantly pounded into M.D.'s-to-be that they must beware of what the patient says about the way he feels. A doctor is taught to pay close attention to the objective "signs" of disease processes, but to take the subjective reports ("symptoms") of the patient with a grain of salt. It is very reasonable to do it this way, because one can deal more readily with what is objective. However, this attitude also has the effect of hiding near-death experiences, since very few physicians make it a practice to ask about the feelings and perceptions of patients whom they resuscitate from clinical death. Because of this attitude, I would guess that doctors—who in theory should be the group most likely to uncover near-death experiences—are in fact not much more likely to hear of near-death experiences than are other persons.

Have you detected any differences between males and females with respect to this phenomenon?

There seems to be no difference at all in the contents or types of experiences reported by males and females. I have found both males and females who have described each of the common aspects of near-death encounters which have been discussed, and there is no one element which seems to weigh either more or less heavily in male vs. female reports.

Still, there are differences between male and female subjects. On the whole, males who have had death experiences are far more reticent to talk about them than are females. Far more males than females have told me briefly of experiences, only to fail to respond to my letters or return my calls when I tried to follow up with a more detailed interview. Many more males than females have made remarks such as "I tried to forget it, suppress it," often alluding to fears of ridicule, or intimating that the emotions involved in the experience were too overwhelming for them to recount.

Although I cannot offer any explanation of why this should be so, apparently I am not alone in noticing it. Dr. Russell Moores, a noted psychical researcher, has told me that he and others have observed the same thing. About one-third as many men as women come to him reporting a psychical experience.

Another interesting fact is that a somewhat larger number of these experiences than would be expected took place during pregnancy. Again, I can't explain why this should be. Perhaps it is only that pregnancy is in itself a rather risky physiological state in many ways, attendant with many potential medical complications. Coupled with the fact that only women get pregnant, and that women are less reticent than men to talk, this might help explain the frequency of experiences taking place during pregnancy.

How do you know that all these people aren't just lying to you?

It is quite easy for persons who have not listened and watched as others have related near-death experiences intellectually to entertain the hypothesis that these stories are lies. However, I find myself in a rather unique position. I have witnessed mature, emotionally stable adults—both men and women—break down and weep while telling me of events that happened up to three decades before. I have detected in their voices sincerity, warmth, and feeling which cannot really be conveyed in a written recounting. So to me, in a way that is unfortunately impossible for many others to share, the notion that these accounts might be fabrications is utterly untenable.

In addition to the weight of my own opinion, there are some strong considerations which should rule heavily against the fabrication hypothesis. The most obvious is the difficulty of explaining the similarity of so many of the accounts. How is it that many people just happen to have come up with the same lie to tell me over a period of eight years? Collusion remains a theoretical possibility here. It is certainly conceivable that a nice elderly lady from eastern North Carolina, a medical student from New Jersey, a Georgia veterinarian, and many others several years ago banded together and conspired to carry out an elaborate hoax against me. However, I don't regard this to be a very likely possibility!

If they are not overtly lying, perhaps they are misrepresenting in a more subtle way. Isn't it possible that over the years, they have elaborated their stories?

This question points to the well-known psychological phenomenon in which a person may start with a fairly simple account of an experience or event and over a period of time develop it into a very elaborate narrative. With each telling, a subtle detail is added, the speaker coming eventually to believe it himself, until at last the story is so embellished as to bear little resemblance to the original.

I do not believe that this mechanism has been operative to any significant degree in the cases I have studied, however. In the first place, the accounts of persons whom I have interviewed very soon after their experience—in some cases, while they were still in the hospital recovering—are of the same type as those of people who have recounted experiences which took place decades

138

ago. Further, in a few cases, persons whom I have interviewed wrote down descriptions of their experiences shortly after they happened and read to me from their notes during the interview. Again, these descriptions are of the same sort as experiences which are recounted from memory after lapses of some years. Also, there is the fact that quite often I have been only the first or second person to whom an experience has been related, and then only with great reluctance, even in cases where the experience happened some years before. Though there has been little or no opportunity for embellishment in such cases, these accounts, again, are no different as a group from those accounts that have been retold more often over a period of years. Finally, it is quite possible that in many cases, the reverse of embellishment has taken place. What psychiatrists call "suppression" is a mental mechanism whereby a conscious effort is made to control undesired memories, feelings, or thoughts or to conceal them from awareness. On numerous occasions in the course of interviews, persons have made remarks which are strongly indicative that suppression has occurred. For example, one woman who reported to me a very elaborate experience which took place during her "death" said, "I feel that there is more to it, but I can't remember it all. I tried to suppress it because I knew people weren't going to believe me anyway." A man who suffered a cardiac arrest

139

during surgery for major wounds received in Viet Nam related his difficulty in dealing with his out-of-body experiences emotionally. "I get choked up by trying to tell about it even now. . . . I feel that there is a lot I don't remember about it. I have tried to forget it." In short, it seems that a strong case can be made that embellishment has not been a very significant factor in the development of these stories.

Did all these people profess a religion before their experiences? If so, aren't the experiences shaped by their religious beliefs and backgrounds?

They seem to be to some extent. As mentioned earlier, though the description of the being of light is invariable, the identity ascribed to it varies, apparently as a function of the religious background of the individual. Through all of my research, however, I have not heard a single reference to a heaven or a hell anything like the customary picture to which we are exposed in this society. Indeed, many persons have stressed how unlike their experiences were to what they had been led to expect in the course of their religious training. One woman who "died" reported: "I had always heard that when you die, you see both heaven and hell, but I didn't see either one." Another lady who had an out-of-body experience after severe injuries said, "The strange thing was that I had always been taught in my religious upbringing that the minute you died you would be right at these beautiful gates, pearly gates. But there I was hovering around my own physical body, and that was it! I was just baffled." Furthermore, in quite a few instances reports have come from persons who had no religious beliefs or training at all prior to their experiences, and their descriptions do not seem to differ in content from people who had quite strong religious beliefs. In a few cases, someone who had been exposed to religious doctrines but had rejected them earlier in life acquired religious feelings with new depth after the experience. Others say that although they had read religious writings, such as *The Bible*, they had never really understood certain things they had read there until their near-death experiences.

What bearing, if any, do the experiences which you have studied have on the possibility of reincarnation?

Not one of the cases I have looked into is in any way indicative to me that reincarnation occurs. However, it is important to bear in mind that not one of them rules out reincarnation, either. If reincarnation does occur, it seems likely that an interlude in some other realm would occur between the time of separation from the old body and the entry into the new one. Accordingly, the technique of interviewing people who come back from close calls with death would not be the proper mode for studying reincarnation, anyway.

Other methods can and have been tried in investigating reincarnation. For example, some have tried the technique of "far age regression." A subject is hypnotized and the suggestion is made to him that he go back mentally to successively earlier and earlier times in his life. When he reaches the time of the earliest experiences he can recall in his present life, he is then told to try to go back even beyond that! At this point, many persons begin telling elaborate stories about previous lives in earlier times and distant places. In some cases, such stories check out with remarkable accuracy. This has happened even when it can be established that the subject could not have known in any normal way about the events, persons, and places he describes so accurately. The case of Bridey Murphy is the most famous, but there are many others, some even more impressive and well-documented, which are not as widely known. Readers who wish to pursue this question further are referred to the excellent study, *Twenty Cases Suggestive of Reincarnation*, by Ian Stevenson, M.D. It is also worth noting that *The Tibetan Book of the Dead*, which so accurately recounts the stages of near-death encounters, says that reincarnation does occur at some later point, after the events which have been related by my subjects.

Have you ever interviewed anyone who has had a near-death experience in association with a suicide attempt? If so, was the experience any different?

I do know of a few cases in which a suicide attempt was the cause of the apparent "death." These experiences were uniformly characterized as being unpleasant.

As one woman said, "If you leave here a tormented soul, you will be a tormented soul over there, too." In short, they report that the conflicts they had attempted suicide to escape were still present when they died, but with added complications. In their disembodied state they were unable to do anything about their problems, and they also had to view the unfortunate consequences which resulted from their acts.

A man who was despondent about the death of his wife shot himself, "died" as a result, and was resuscitated. He states:

> I didn't go where [my wife] was. I went to an awful place. . . . I immediately saw the mistake I had made. . . . I thought, "I wish I hadn't done it."

Others who experienced this unpleasant "limbo" state have remarked that they had the feeling they would be there for a long time. This was their penalty for "breaking the rules" by trying to release themselves prematurely from what was, in effect, an "assignment"—to fulfill a certain purpose in life.

Such remarks coincide with what has been reported to me by several people who "died" of other causes but who said that, while they were in this state, it had been intimated to them that suicide was a very unfortunate act which attended with a severe penalty. One man who had a near-death experience after an accident said:

[While I was over there] I got the feeling that two things it was completely forbidden for me to do would be to kill myself or to kill another person. . . . If I were to commit suicide, I would be throwing God's gift back in his face. . . . Killing somebody else would be interfering with God's purpose for that individual.

Sentiments like these, which by now have been expressed to me in many separate accounts, are identical to those embodied in the most ancient theological and moral argument against suicide— one which occurs in various forms in the writings of thinkers as diverse as St. Thomas Aquinas, Locke, and Kant. A suicide, in Kant's view, is acting in opposition to the purposes of God and arrives on the other side viewed as a rebel against his creator. Aquinas argues that life is a gift from God and that it is God's prerogative, not man's, to take it back.

In discussing this, however, I do not pass a moral judgment against suicide. I only report what others who have been through this experience have told me. I am now in the process of preparing a second book on near-death experiences, in which this topic, along with others, will be dealt with at greater length.

Do you have any cross-cultural cases?

No, I don't. In fact, one of the many reasons I say that my study is not "scientific" is that the group of individuals to whom I have listened is not a random sample of human beings. I would be very interested in hearing about the near-death experiences of Eskimos, Kwakiutl Indians, Navahos, Watusi tribesmen, and so on. However, due to geographic and other limitations, I have not been able to locate any.

Are there any historical examples of near-death phenomena?

As far as I know, there are not. However, since I have been fully occupied with contemporary instances, I have simply not had the time adequately to research this question. So I would not at all be surprised to find that such reports have been recounted in the past. On the other hand, I strongly suspect that near-death experiences have been vastly more common in the past few decades than in earlier periods. The reason for this is simply that it has only been in fairly recent times that advanced resuscitation technology has been available. Many of the people who have been brought back in our era would not have survived in earlier years. Injections of adrenalin into the heart, a machine which delivers a shock to the heart, and artificial heart and lung machines are examples of such medical advances.

Have you investigated the medical records of your subjects?

In so far as possible, I have. In the cases I have been invited to investigate, the records have borne out the assertions of the persons involved. In some cases, due to the passage of time and/or the death of the persons who carried out the resuscitation, records are not available. The reports for which substantiating records are not available are no different from those in which records are available. In many instances when medical records have not been accessible, I have secured the testimony of others—friends, doctors, or relatives of the informant—to the effect that the near-death event did occur.

I have heard that, after five minutes, resuscitation is impossible, yet you say that some of your cases have been "dead" for up to twenty minutes. How is this possible?

Most numbers and quantities one hears quoted in medical practice are means, averages, and are not to be taken as absolutes. The figure of five minutes which one often hears quoted is an average. It is a clinical rule of thumb not to attempt resuscitation after five minutes because, in most instances, brain damage from lack of oxygen would have occurred beyond that time. However, since it is only an average, one would expect individual cases to fall on either side of it. I have in fact found cases in which resuscitation took place after twenty minutes with no evidence of brain damage.

Were any of these people really dead?

One of the main reasons why this question is so confusing and difficult to answer is that it is partly a semantic question involving the meaning of the word "dead." As the recent heated controversy surrounding the transplantation of organs reveals, the definition of "death" is by no means settled, even among professionals in the field of medicine. Criteria of death vary not only between laymen and physicians, but also among physicians and from hospital to hospital. So, the answer to this question will depend on what is meant by "dead." It will be profitable here to look at three definitions in turn and to comment upon them.

1. "DEATH" AS THE ABSENCE OF CLINICALLY DETECTABLE VITAL SIGNS.

Some will be willing to say that a person is "dead" if his heart stops beating and he quits breathing for an extended period of time, his blood pressure drops as low as to be unreadable, his pupils dilate, his body temperature begins to go down, etc. This is the clinical definition, and it has been employed for centuries by physicians and laymen alike. In fact, most people who have ever been pronounced dead were adjudged so on the basis of this criterion.

There is no question but that this clinical standard was met in many of the cases I have studied. Both the testimony of physicians and the evidence of medical records adequately support the contention that "deaths" in this sense did take place.

2. "DEATH" AS THE ABSENCE OF BRAIN WAVE ACTIVITY.

The advancement of technology has brought the development of more sensitive techniques for detecting biological processes, even those which might not be observable overtly. The electroencephalograph (EEG) is a machine which amplifies and records the minute electrical potentials of the brain. Recently, the trend has been to base assessment of "real" death on the absence of electrical activity in the brain, as determined by the presence of "flat" EEG tracings.

Obviously, in all of the cases of resuscitation which I have dealt with, there was an extreme clinical emergency. There was no time to set up an EEG; the clinicians were rightly concerned about doing what they could to get their patient back. So, some might argue that none of these persons can be adjudged to have been "dead."

Suppose for a moment, however, that "flat" EEG readings had been obtained on a large percentage of the persons who were thought dead and were then resuscitated. Would that fact necessarily add very much here? I think not, for three reasons. First, resuscitation attempts are always emergencies, which last at the very most for thirty minutes or so. Setting up an EEG machine is a very complicated and technical task, and it is fairly common for even an experienced technician to have to work with it for some time to get correct readings, even under optimum conditions. In an emergency, with its accompanying confusion, there would probably be an increased likelihood of mistakes. So, even if one could present a flat EEG tracing for a person who told of a near-death experience, it would still be possible for a critic to say—with justice—that the tracing might not be accurate.

Second, even the marvelous electric brain machine, properly set up, does not enable us infallibly to determine whether resuscitation is possible in any given case. Flat EEG tracings have been obtained in persons who were later resuscitated. Overdoses of drugs which are depressants of the central nervous system, as well as hypothermia (low body temperature) have both resulted in this phenomenon.

Third, even if I could produce a case in which it could be established that the machine was correctly set up, there would still be a problem. Someone could say that there is no proof that the reported near-death experience took place during the time the EEG was flat, but rather before or afterwards. I conclude, then, that the EEG is not very valuable at this present stage of investigation.

3. "DEATH" AS AN IRREVERSIBLE LOSS OF VITAL FUNCTIONS.

Others will adopt an even more restricted definition, holding that one cannot say that a person was ever "dead," no matter how long his vital signs were clinically undetectable, and no matter how long his EEG was flat, if he was subsequently resuscitated. In other words, "death" is defined as that state of the body from which it is impossible to be revived. Obviously, by this definition, none of my cases would qualify, since they all involved resuscitation.

We have seen, then, that the answer to the question depends upon what is meant by "dead." One must remember that even though this is in part a semantic dispute, it is nonetheless an important issue, because all three definitions embody important insights. In fact, I would agree with the third, most stringent definition to some extent. Even in those cases in which the heart was not beating for extended periods, the tissues of the body, particularly the brain, must somehow have been perfused (supplied with oxygen and nourishment) most of the time. It is not necessary that one assume in any of these cases that any law of biology or physiology was violated. In order for resuscitation to have occurred, some degree of residual biological activity must have been going on in the cells of the body, even though the overt signs of these processes were not clinically detectable by the methods employed. However, it seems that it is impossible at present to determine exactly what the point of no return is. It may well vary with the individual, and it is likely not a fixed point but rather a shifting range on a continuum. In fact, a few decades ago most of the people with whom I have talked could not have been brought back. In the future, techniques might become available which would enable us to revive people who can't be saved today.

Let us, therefore, hypothesize that death is a separation of the mind from the body, and that the mind does pass into other realms of existence at this point. It would follow that there exists some mechanism whereby the soul or mind is released upon death. One has no basis upon which to assume, though, that this mechanism works exactly in accordance with what we have in our own era somewhat arbitrarily taken to be the point of no return. Nor do we have to assume that it works perfectly in every instance, any more than we have to assume that any bodily system always works perfectly. Perhaps this mechanism might sometime come into play even before any physiological crisis, affording a few persons a brief glimpse of other realities. This would help to account for the reports of those persons who have had flashbacks of their lives, out-of-body experiences, etc., when they felt certain that they were about to be killed, even before any physical injury occurred.

All I ultimately want to claim is this: Whatever

that point of irretrievable death is said to be—whether in the past, present, or future—those with whom I have talked have been much closer to it than have the vast majority of their fellow human beings. For this reason alone, I am quite willing to listen to what they have to say.

In the final analysis, though, it is quite pointless to cavil over the precise definition of "death"—irreversible or otherwise—in the context of this discussion. What the person who raises such objections to near-death experiences seems to have in mind is something more basic. He reasons that as long as it remains a possibility that there was some residual biological activity in the body, then that activity might have caused, and thus account for, the experience.

Now, I granted earlier that there must have been some residual biological function in the body in all cases. So, the issue of whether a "real" death occurred really reduces to the more basic problem of whether the residual biological function could account for the occurrence of the experiences. In other words:

Aren't other explanations (i.e., other than survival of bodily death) possible?

This in turn brings us to the topic of the next chapter.

152

5
EXPLANATIONS

Of course alternative "explanations" of near-death phenomena are available. In fact, from the purely philosophical point of view, an infinity of hypotheses could be constructed to explain any experience, observation, or fact. That is, one could go on forever manufacturing more and more theoretically possible explanations for anything one wanted to explain. It is the same in the case of near-death experiences; all sorts of possible explanations present themselves.

Out of the many kinds of explanations which might theoretically be proposed, there are a few which have been suggested quite frequently in the audiences which I have addressed. Accordingly, I shall now deal with these more common explanations, and with another which, though it has never been proposed to me, might well have been. I have somewhat arbitrarily divided them into three types: Supernatural, Natural (Scientific), and Psychological.

155

Supernatural Explanations

Rarely, someone in one of my audiences has proposed demonic explanations of near-death experiences, suggesting that the experiences were doubtless directed by inimical forces. As a response to such explanations, I can only say this. It seems to me that the best way of distinguishing between God-directed and Satan-directed experiences would be to see what the person involved does and says after his experience. God, I suppose, would try to get those to whom he appears to be loving and forgiving. Satan would presumably tell his servants to follow a course of hate and destruction. Manifestly, my subjects have come back with a renewed commitment to follow the former course and to disavow the latter. In the light of all the machinations which a hypothetical demon would have to have carried out in order to delude his hapless victim (and to what purpose?), he certainly has failed miserably—as far as I can tell—to make persuasive emissaries for his program!

Natural (Scientific) Explanations

1. THE PHARMACOLOGICAL EXPLANATION

Some suggest that near-death experiences are caused by the therapeutic drugs administered to the person at the time of his crisis. The surface plausibility of this view derives from several facts. For example, it is generally agreed by most medical scientists and laymen that certain drugs cause delusional and hallucinatory mental states and experiences. Furthermore, we are now passing through an era in which there is intense interest in the problem of drug abuse, and much public attention has focused on the illicit use of drugs such as LSD, marijuana, and so forth, which do appear to cause such hallucinatory episodes. Finally, there is the fact that even many medically-accepted drugs are associated with various effects on the mind which may resemble the events of the experience of dying. For example, the drug ketamine (or cyclohexanone) is an intravenously injected anesthetic with side effects which are similar in some respects to out-of-body experiences. It is classified as a "dissociative" anesthetic because during induction the patient may become unresponsive not only to pain but also to the environment as a whole. He feels "dissociated" from his environment, including the parts of his own body —his legs, arms, and so forth. For a time after recovery, he may be left with psychological disturbances, including hallucinations and very vivid dreams. (Note that a few persons have used this very word—"dissociation"—to characterize their feelings while in the out-of-body state.)

What is more, I have collected a few accounts from people who, while under anesthetics, had what they plainly identified as hallucinatory-type visions of death. Let me give one example.

It was some time in my early teen-age years, I was in the dentist's office for a filling and was given nitrous oxide. I was kind of nervous about taking it, because I was afraid I wouldn't wake up again. As the anesthesia began to take effect, I felt myself going around in a spiral. It wasn't like I was turning around, but like the dentist's chair was moving in a spiral upward, and it was going up and up and up.

Everything was very bright and white and as I got to the top of the spiral, angels came down to meet me and to take me to heaven. I use the plural, "angels," because it's very vague but I'm sure that there were more than one. Yet I can't say how many.

At one point the dentist and nurse were talking to each other about another person, and I heard them, but by the time they finished a sentence I couldn't even remember what the first of the sentence had been. But I knew they were talking, and as they did their words would echo around and around. It was an echo that seemed to get further and further away, like in the mountains. I do remember that I seemed to hear them from above, because I felt as though I was up high, going to heaven.

That's all I remember except that I hadn't been afraid or panicked at the thought of dying. At that time in my life, I was afraid of going to hell, but when this happened there was no question in my mind but that I was going to heaven. I was very surprised later that the thought of death hadn't bothered me, but finally it dawned on me

158

that in my anesthetized state nothing bothered me. The whole thing was just happy because I'm sure the gas made me completely carefree. I blamed it on that. It was such a vague thing. I didn't dwell on it afterwards.

Notice that there are a few points of similarity between this experience and some others which have been taken to be real by those to whom they happened. This woman describes a brilliant white light, meeting others who are there to take her to the other side, and lack of concern over being dead. There are also two aspects which suggest an out-of-body experience: Her impression that she heard the voices of the dentist and nurse from a position above them, and her feeling of "floating."

On the other hand, other details of this story are very atypical of near-death experiences which are reported as having actually happened. The brilliant light is not personified and no ineffable feelings of peace and happiness occurred. The description of the after-death world is very literalistic and, she says, in accordance with her religious training. The beings who met her are identified as "angels," and she talks of going to a "heaven" which is located in the "up" direction, where she is headed. She denies seeing her body or being in any other kind of body, and she plainly feels that the dentist's chair, and not her own motion, was the source of the rotatory movement. She repeatedly stresses the vagueness of her experience, and it apparently had no effect on her belief in an afterlife. (In fact, she now has doubts about survival of bodily death.)

In comparing reports in which the experience is plainly attributed to a drug with near-death experiences which are reported as real, several points need to be mentioned. First of all, the few people who have described such "drug" experiences to me are no more and no less romantic, imaginative, intelligent, or stable than are the persons reporting "real" near-death experiences. Secondly, these drug-induced experiences are extremely vague. Thirdly, the stories vary among themselves, and also markedly from the "real" near-death visions. I should say that in choosing the specific case of the "anesthetic" type of experience to be used, I have purposefully chosen the one which *most closely resembles* the group of "real" experiences. So, I would suggest that there are, in general, very great differences between these two types of experiences.

Furthermore, there are many additional factors which rule against the pharmacological explanation of near-death phenomena. The most significant one is simply that in many cases no drug had been administered prior to the experience nor, in some cases, were drugs given even after the near-death event. In fact, many persons have made it a point to insist to me that the experience clearly took place before any kind of medication was given, in some cases long before they obtained any sort of medical attention. Even in those instances in which therapeutic drugs were administered around the time of the near-death event, the variety of drugs employed for different patients is enormous. They range from substances such as aspirin through antibiotics and the hormone adrenalin to local and gaseous anesthetics. Most of these drugs are not associated with central nervous system or psychic effects. It also should be noted that there are no differences as groups between the experiences related by those who were given no drugs at all and the experiences related by those who were under medications of various types. Finally, I shall note without comment that one woman who "died" twice on separate occasions some years apart attributed her *lack* of an experience the first time to her anesthetized condition. The second time, when she was under no drugs at all, she had a very complex experience.

One of the assumptions of modern medical pharmacology is the notion, which also seems to have gained acceptance among the great mass of laymen in our society, that psychoactive drugs *cause* the psychic episodes with which their use is associated. These psychic events are therefore considered to be "unreal," "hallucinatory," "delusional," or "only in the mind." One must remember, however, that this view is by no means universally accepted; there is another view of the relationship between drugs and experiences attending their use. I refer to the initiatory and exploratory use of

161

what we call "hallucinogenic" drugs. Through the ages men have turned to such psychoactive compounds in their quest to achieve other states of consciousness and to reach other planes of reality. (For a lively and fascinating contemporary exposition of this side of drug use, see the recent book, *The Natural Mind*, by Andrew Weil, M.D.) Thus, drug use has historically been associated, not only with medicine and the treatment of disease, but also with religion and the attainment of enlightenment. For example, in the well-publicized rituals of the peyote cult found among American Indians in the western United States, the peyote cactus plant (which contains the substance mescaline) is ingested in order to attain religious visions and enlightenment. There are similar cults all over the world, and their members share the belief that the drug they employ provides a means of passage into other dimensions of reality. Assuming this viewpoint to be valid, it could be hypothesized that drug use would be only one pathway among many leading to the achievement of enlightenment and to the discovery of other realms of existence. The experience of dying could, then, be another such pathway, and all this would help to account for the resemblance of drug-induced experiences like the one given above to near-death experiences.

2. PHYSIOLOGICAL EXPLANATIONS

Physiology is that branch of biology which

deals with the functions of the cells, organs and whole bodies of living beings, and with the inter-relationships among these functions. A physiological explanation of near-death phenomena which I have often heard proposed is that, since the oxygen supply to the brain is cut off during clinical death and some other kinds of severe bodily stress, the phenomena perceived must represent some sort of last compensatory gasp of the dying brain.

The main thing wrong with this hypothesis is simply this: As can easily be seen from a survey of the dying experiences reported earlier, many of the near-death experiences happened before any physiological stress of the required type took place. Indeed, in a few cases there was no bodily injury at all during the encounter. Yet, every single element which appears in cases of severe injury can also be seen in other instances in which injury was not involved.

3. NEUROLOGICAL EXPLANATIONS

Neurology is the medical specialty dealing with the cause, diagnosis, and treatment of diseases of the nervous system (that is the brain, spinal cord, and nerves). Phenomena similar to those reported by persons who nearly die show up also in certain neurological conditions. So, some might propose neurological explanations of near-death experiences in terms of supposed malfunctions in the nervous system of the dying person. Let us

163

consider neurological parallels for two of the more striking events of the dying experience: The instantaneous "review" of the events of the dying person's life and the out-of-body phenomenon.

I encountered a patient on the neurology ward at a hospital who described a peculiar form of seizure disorder in which he saw flashbacks of events in his earlier life.

The first time it happened, I was looking at a friend of mine across the room. The right side of his face just kind of became distorted. All of a sudden, there was an intrusion into my consciousness of scenes of things that had happened in the past. They were just like they were when they actually happened—vivid, completely in color, and three-dimensional. I felt nauseated, and I was so startled that I tried to avoid the images. Since then, I've had many of these attacks, and I've learned just to let it run its course. The closest parallel I can draw to it is the films they have on television at New Year's. Scenes of things that happened that year are flashed on the screen and when you see one, it's gone before you can really think about it. That's how it is with these attacks. I'll see something and think, "Oh, I remember that." And I'll try to keep it in my mind, but another is flashed up before I can.

The images are things that really happened. Nothing is modified. When it is over, though, it is very difficult to recall what images I saw. Sometimes, it's the same images, other times not. As they appear I remember, "Oh, these are the same ones I've seen before," but when it's over it's almost impossible to recall what they were. They don't seem to be particularly significant events in my life. In fact, none of them are. They all seem very trivial. They don't happen in any sort of order, not even in the order they happened in my life. They just come at random.

When the images come, I can still see what's going on around me, but my awareness is diminished. I'm not as sharp. It's almost as if half of my mind is taken up with the images, and the other half is on what I'm doing. People who have seen me during an attack say that it just lasts about a minute, but to me it seems like ages.

There are certain obvious similarities between these seizures, which doubtless were occasioned by a focus of irritation in the brain, and the panoramic memory reported by some of my near-death subjects. For example, this man's seizure took the form of visual images which were incredibly vivid and were actually three-dimensional. Further, the images just seemed to come to him, quite apart from any intention on his part. He also reports that the images came with great rapidity and he emphasizes the distortion of his senses of time which went along with the seizure.

On the other hand, there are striking differences as well. Unlike those seen in near-death experiences, the memory images did not come in the order of his life, nor were they seen all at once, in a unifying vision. They were not highlights or significant events in his life; he stresses their triviality. Thus, they did not seem to be presented to him for judgmental or educational purposes. While many near-death subjects point out that after their "review" they could remember the events of their life with much greater clarity and in more detail than before, this man states that he could not remember what the particular images were following the seizure.

Out-of-body experiences have a neurological analogue in so-called "autoscopic (self-seeing) hallucinations," which are the subject of an excellent article by Dr. N. Lukianowicz in the medical journal, *Archives of Neurology and Psychiatry*. In these odd visions, the subject sees a projection of himself into his own visual field. This strange "double" mimicks the facial expressions and other bodily movements of its original, who is completely baffled and confused when he suddenly sees an image of himself at a distance from himself, usually straight ahead.

Though this experience is clearly somewhat analogous to the out-of-body visions described earlier, the differences heavily outweigh the similarities. The autoscopic phantom is always perceived as alive—sometimes it is thought of by the subject as even more alive and conscious than he is—while in out-of-body experiences the body is seen as something lifeless, just a shell. The autoscopic subject may "hear" his double talk to him, give him instructions, taunt him, and so on. While in out-of-body experiences the whole body is seen (unless it is partly covered up or otherwise concealed), the autoscopic double is far more frequently seen only from the chest or neck up.

In fact, autoscopic copies have many more features in common with what I have called the spiritual body than with the physical body which is seen by a dying person. Autoscopic doubles, though sometimes seen in color, are more often described as wispy, transparent, and colorless. The subject may in fact see his image walk through doors or other physical obstacles without any apparent trouble.

I present here an account of an apparent autoscopic hallucination which was described to me. It is unique in that it involved two persons simultaneously.

About eleven o'clock one summer night about two years before my wife and I were married, I was driving her home in my sports convertible. I parked the car on the dimly-lit street in front of her house, and we were both surprised as we both looked up at the same time and saw huge images of ourselves, from the waist up and sitting side by side, in the big trees which hung over the street about one hundred feet directly ahead of us. The images were dark, almost like silhouettes, and we couldn't see through them at all, but they were quite exact replicas, anyway. Neither of us had any trouble recognizing both of them at once. They moved around, but not in imitation of our movements, since we were just sitting still watching them. They did things such as: My image picked up a book and showed something in it to the image of my wife, and she leaned over and looked more closely at the book.

As we sat there, I would narrate the scene for a while—tell my wife what I saw the images doing—and what I said was exactly what she had been seeing them doing. Then we would switch. She would tell me what she was seeing them doing, and it would be exactly what I had seen.

We sat there for a long time—at least thirty minutes—watching this and talking about it as we watched it. I guess we could have gone on like that for the rest of the night. My wife had to go in, though, so we finally just walked together up the steps going up the hill to her house. When I came back down, I saw the images again, and they were still there as I drove away.

There is no chance that this was any sort of reflection of us in the windshield because the top of the car was down and we were looking way up over the windshield to see them the whole time. Neither of us ever drank, either—and we still don't—and this was three years before we had even heard anything about LSD or drugs like that. We weren't tired, either, even though it was fairly late, so we weren't asleep and dreaming it. We were very awake, alert, amazed, and excited as we watched the images and talked about them with each other.

Granted, autoscopic hallucinations are in some ways like the out-of-body phenomenon associated with a near-death experience. However, even if we were to focus on all the points of similarity and to neglect the differences entirely, the existence of autoscopic hallucinations would not give us an explanation for the occurrence of out-of-body experiences. The simple reason is that there is no explanation for autoscopic hallucinations, either. Many conflicting explanations have been proposed by different neurologists and psychiatrists, but they are still debated, and no one theory has gained general acceptance. So, to try to explain all out-of-body experiences as autoscopic hallucinations would only be to substitute a bafflement for an enigma.

Finally, there is another point which is relevant to the discussion of neurological explanations for near-death experiences. In one case I found a subject who had a residual neurological problem deriving from a near-death encounter. The problem was a very mild deficit consisting of the partial paralysis of a small group of muscles on one side of the body. Though I have often asked whether there were any residual deficits, this is the only example I have found of neurological damage following a near-death encounter.

Psychological Explanations

Psychology has not yet attained anything approaching the degree of rigor and precision which some other sciences have reached in the modern age. Psychologists are still divided into contesting schools of thought with conflicting viewpoints, investigative approaches, and fundamental understandings about the existence and nature of the mind. Psychological explanations of near-death experiences, therefore, will vary widely according to the school of thought to which the explainer belongs. Instead of considering each type of psychological explanation which might possibly be proposed, I shall stick to a few which I have heard most often from members of my audience, and to one which has struck me as in a way the most tempting.

I touched earlier on two commonly proposed psychological type explanations—those which hypothesize that either conscious lying or unconscious embellishment might have occurred. In the present chapter I want to consider two others.

1. ISOLATION RESEARCH

In all of the public lectures I have presented on my studies, no one has ever advanced an explanation of near-death experiences in terms of the results of isolation research. Yet it is in precisely this relatively recent and rapidly growing area of behavioral science that phenomena most closely resembling the stages of the experience of dying have been studied and produced under laboratory conditions.

Isolation research is the study of what happens to the mind and body of a person who is isolated in one way or another; for example, by being removed from all social contact with other humans, or by being subjected to a monotonous, repetitive task for long periods.

Data on situations of this type has been gathered in several ways. Written accounts of the experiences of lone polar explorers or of solitary survivors of shipwrecks contain much information. During the last few decades, researchers have attempted to investigate similar phenomena under laboratory conditions. One well-publicized technique has been to suspend a volunteer in a tank of water which is the same temperature as his body. This minimizes sensations of weight and temperature. He is blindfolded and his ears are fitted with plugs to intensify the effect of the dark, sound-proofed tank. His arms are constrained in tubes so that he cannot move them, and he is thus deprived of many of the normal sensations of joint movement and position.

Under these and other solitary conditions, some people have experienced unusual psychological phenomena, many of which strongly resemble those I outlined in Chapter 2. One woman who spent long periods alone in the desolate conditions of the North Pole reports a panoramic vision of the events of her life. Shipwrecked sailors stranded alone in small boats for many weeks have described hallucinations of being rescued, sometimes by paranormal beings almost like ghosts or spirits. This bears vague analogies to the being of light or departed spirits whom many of my subjects

have encountered. Other near-death type phenomena which recur in accounts of isolation experiences include: Distortions of sense of time,
feelings of being partly dissociated from the body,
resistance to going back to civilization or leaving
isolation, and feelings of being "at one" with the
universe. In addition, many who have been isolated by shipwreck or other such events say that
after a few weeks of being in this condition, they
came back to civilization with a profound change
of values. They may report that afterwards they
feel inwardly more secure. Clearly, this reinte-
gration of personality is similar to that claimed by
many who have come back from death.

Likewise, there are certain aspects of dying situations that are much like the features found in isolation experiences and studies. Patients who come
near death are often isolated and immobile in the
recovery rooms of hospitals, often in conditions
of subdued sound and light and with no visitors.
One might even wonder whether the physiological changes associated with the death of the body
could produce a radical kind of isolation resulting
in an almost total cut-off of sensory input to the
brain. Further, as was discussed at length earlier,
many near-death patients have told me of the dis-
tressing feelings of isolation, of loneliness, and of
being cut off from human contact which came
over them when they were out of their bodies.

Indeed, one could no doubt find borderline cases
which could not be classified clearly either as

near-death experiences or as isolation experiences. For example, one man gave me the following story of his stay in the hospital during a severe illness.

> I was extremely ill in the hospital, and as I lay there I kept seeing pictures coming at me, just as though they were on a television screen. The pictures were of people, and I could see a person, as though out in space at a distance, and it would start coming toward me, then it would go past and another one would appear. I was perfectly aware that I was in the hospital room and was sick, but I started to wonder what was going on. Now, some of these people I knew personally—they were friends and relatives of mine—but the others I didn't know. Suddenly, I realized that all the ones I knew were people who had died.

One might well ask how to classify this experience, since it has points of similarity to both near-death and isolation experiences. It seems somewhat analogous to the near-death experiences in which meetings with the spirits of departed individuals took place, and yet different from them in that no other near-death phenomena took place. Interestingly, in one isolation study a subject, who was alone in a cubicle for some time, described hallucinations in which he saw pictures of famous men drifting past him. So, is the experience just quoted to be classified as a near-death experience occasioned by the patient's extreme illness, or as an isolation experience brought on by the conditions of confinement necessitated by the state of his health? It might even be the case that no absolute criteria can be drawn up which would enable one to classify every such experience into one of the two separate categories. Perhaps there will always be borderline cases.

Despite these overlaps, however, the results of isolation research do not provide a satisfactory explanation for near-death experiences. In the first place, the diverse mental phenomena occurring in conditions of isolation cannot themselves be explained by any current theory. To appeal to isolation studies to explain near-death experiences would be, as in the case of "explaining" out-of-body experiences by referring to autoscopic hallucinations, merely to substitute one mystery for another. For, there are two conflicting strains of thought about the nature of the visions which take place in conditions of isolation. Some no doubt take them as "unreal" and "hallucinatory," and yet all throughout history mystics and shamans have sought solitude in the wilderness in order to find enlightenment and revelation. The notion that spiritual rebirth can be brought about by isolation is an integral part of the belief systems of many cultures and is reflected in many great religious writings, including *The Bible*.

Although this idea is somewhat alien to our contemporary Western belief structure, there are still numerous proponents of it, even in our own society. One of the earliest and most influential isolation researchers, John Lilly, M.D., has recently written a book, a spiritual autobiography, entitled *The Center of the Cyclone*. In this book he makes it clear that he regards the experiences he had under conditions of isolation to be real experiences of enlightenment and insight, and not "unreal" or "delusional" at all. It is also interesting to note that he recounts a near-death experience of his own which is very much like the ones with which I have dealt, and that he puts his near-death experiences in the same category with his isolation experiences. Isolation, therefore, may very well be, along with hallucinatory drugs and a close call with death, one of several ways of entering new realms of consciousness.

2. DREAMS, HALLUCINATIONS, AND DELUSIONS

Perhaps, some say, near-death experiences are only wish-fulfilling dreams, fantasies, or hallucinations which are brought into play by different factors—drugs in one case, cerebral anoxia in another, isolation in yet another, and so on. So, they would explain near-death experiences as delusions.

I think several factors weigh against this. First, consider the great similarity in content and progression we find among the descriptions, despite the fact that what is most generally reported is manifestly not what is commonly imagined, in our cultural milieu, to happen to the dead. In addition, we find that the picture of the events of dying which emerges from these accounts corresponds in a striking way with that painted in very an-

175

cient and esoteric writings totally unfamiliar to my subjects.

Secondly, there remains the fact that the persons with whom I have talked are not victims of psychoses. They have struck me as emotionally stable, normal people who are functional in society. They hold jobs and positions of importance and carry them out responsibly. They have stable marriages and are involved with their families and friends. Almost no one with whom I have talked has had more than one uncanny experience in the course of his life. And, most significantly, these informants are people who can distinguish between dreams and waking experience.

Yet, they are people who report what they underwent as they came near death, not as dreams, but as events which happened to them. They almost invariably assure me in the course of their narratives that their experiences were not dreams, but rather were definitely, emphatically real.

Finally, there is the fact that independent corroboration of a kind exists for certain of the reports of out-of-body episodes. Though commitments to others prevent me from giving names and identifying details, I have seen and heard enough to say that I continue to be baffled and amazed. It is my opinion that anyone looking into near-death experiences in an organized way is likely also to uncover such strange apparent corroboration. At least, I believe he will find enough facts to make him wonder whether near-death experiences, far from being dreams, might not belong in a very different category indeed.

As a final note here, let me point out that "explanations" are not just abstract intellectual systems. They are also in some respects projects of the egos of the persons who hold them. People become emotionally wedded, as it were, to the canons of scientific explanation which they devise or adopt.

In my numerous lectures on my collection of narratives of near-death events, I have encountered proponents of many types of explanations. Persons who are physiologically-, pharmacologically-, or neurologically-minded will regard their own orientations as sources of explanations which are intuitively obvious, even when cases are brought up which seem to weigh against that particular explanation. Those who espouse the theories of Freud delight in seeing the being of light as a projection of the subject's father, while Jungians see archetypes of the collective unconscious, and so on *ad infinitum*.

Although I want to emphasize again that I am not proposing any new explanations of my own through all this, I have tried to give a few reasons why explanations that are often proposed seem to me at least questionable. In fact, all I really want to suggest is this: Let us at least leave open the possibility that near-death experiences represent a novel phenomenon for which we may have to devise new modes of explanation and interpretation.

6

IMPRESSIONS

In writing this book I have been acutely conscious that my purpose and perspectives might very easily be misunderstood. In particular, I would like to say to scientifically-minded readers that I am fully aware that what I have done here does not constitute a scientific study. And to my fellow philosophers I would insist that I am not under the delusion that I have "proven" there is life after death. To deal with these matters thoroughly would involve the discussion of technical details which lie beyond the scope of this book, so I shall limit myself to the following brief remarks.

In such specialized studies as logic, law, and science the words "conclusion," "evidence," and "proof" are technical terms and have more sophisticated meanings than they do in common usage. In everyday language these same words are used very loosely. A glance at any of the more sensational popular magazines will enable one to see that almost any unlikely tale will be given as "proof" of some improbable claim.

In logic what can and cannot be said to follow from a given set of premises is not at all a casual matter. It is very vigorously and precisely defined by rules, conventions, and laws. When one says that one has drawn a certain "conclusion," one is implicitly making the claim that anyone who begins from the same premises must arrive at the same conclusion, unless he has made a mistake in logic.

These remarks indicate why I refuse to draw any "conclusions" from my study and why I say that I am not trying to construct a proof of the ancient doctrine of the survival of bodily death. Yet I think that these reports of near-death experiences are very significant. What I want to do is find some middle way of interpreting them—a way which neither rejects these experiences on the basis that they do not constitute scientific or logical proof nor sensationalizes them by resorting to vague emotional claims that they "prove" that there is life after death.

At the same time, it seems to me to be an open possibility that our present inability to construct a "proof" may not represent a limitation imposed by the nature of the near-death experiences themselves. Perhaps it is instead a limitation of the currently accepted modes of scientific and logical thought. It may be that the perspective of scientists and logicians of the future will be very different. (One must remember that historically logic and scientific methodology have not been fixed and static systems but growing, dynamic processes.)

So I am left, not with conclusions or evidence or proofs, but with something much less definite —feelings, questions, analogies, puzzling facts to be explained. In fact, it might be more appropriate to ask, not what conclusions I have drawn on the basis of my study, but rather how the study has affected me personally. In response I can only say: There is something very persuasive about seeing a person describe his experience which cannot easily be conveyed in writing. Their near-death experiences were very real events to these people, and through my association with them the experiences have become real events to me.

I realize, however, that this is a psychological consideration and not a logical one. Logic is a public matter, and psychological considerations are not public in the same way. One person may be affected or changed in one way and another person in a different way by the same set of circumstances. It is a matter of disposition and temperament, and I do not wish to imply that my own reaction to this study should be a law for the thinking of everyone else. In view of this, some might ask, "If the interpretation of these experiences is ultimately such a subjective matter, why study them?" I can think of no other way to answer this than to point again to the universal human concern with the nature of death. I believe that any light whatever which can be shed on the nature of death is to the good.

Enlightenment on this subject is needed by members of many professions and academic fields. It is needed by the physician who has to deal with the fears and hopes of the dying patient and by the minister helping others to face death. It is needed also by psychologists and psychiatrists, because in order to devise a workable and reliable method for the therapy of emotional disturbances they need to know what the mind *is* and whether it can exist apart from the body. If it cannot, then the emphasis of psychological therapy would shift ultimately toward physical methods—drugs, electric shock therapy, brain surgery, and the like. On the other hand, if there are indications that the mind can exist apart from the body and that it is something in its own right, then therapy for mental disorders must finally be something very different.

However, more than academic and professional issues are involved. It involves deeply personal issues, for what we learn about death may make an important difference in the way we live our lives. If experiences of the type which I have discussed are real, they have very profound implications for what every one of us is doing with his life. For, then it would be true that we cannot fully understand this life until we catch a glimpse of what lies beyond it.

BIBLIOGRAPHY

EVANS-WENTZ, W. Y. (ed.), *The Tibetan Book of the Dead*, New York, Oxford University Press, 1957.

HAMILTON, EDITH and CAIRNS, HUNTINGTON (eds.), *The Collected Dialogues of Plato*, New York, Bollingen Foundation, 1961.

LILLY, JOHN C., M.D., *The Center of the Cyclone*, New York, The Julian Press, 1972.

LUKIANOWICZ, N., "Autoscopic Hallucinations," *Archives of Neurology and Psychiatry* (August, 1958).

PLATO, *The Last Days of Socrates*, trans. by Hugh Tredennick, Baltimore, Penguin Books, 1959.

STEVENSON, IAN, M.D., *Twenty Cases Suggestive of Reincarnation*, Charlottesville, University Press of Virginia, 1974.

SWEDENBORG, EMANUEL, *Compendium of the Theological and Spiritual Writings of Emanuel Swedenborg*, Boston, Crosby and Nichols, 1853.

WEIL, ANDREW, M.D., *The Natural Mind*, Boston, Houghton Mifflin, 1973.

ABOUT THE AUTHOR

RAYMOND A. MOODY is married and has two sons. He has studied and taught philosophy extensively, taking a special interest in ethics, logic and the philosophy of language. After having taught philosophy, he continued his studies in medicine and decided to become a psychiatrist in order to teach the philosophy of medicine in a medical school. During this time, he studied the phenomena of survival of bodily death, lecturing to various nursing and medical groups. Because the serious investigation of survival of bodily death is so new, Dr. Moody was unaware that similar research was being conducted by other doctors. It was with the prepublication copy of *Life After Life* that he was brought together with Dr. Elisabeth Kubler-Ross, whose research not only paralleled his own, but *duplicated* his findings. The two had not met before February 1976.

Heartwarming Books
of
Faith and Inspiration

☐	THE GOSPEL ACCORDING TO PEANUTS Robert L. Short	2070 ●	$1.25
☐	BLESS THIS HOUSE Anita Bryant	2568 ●	$1.50
☐	THE TRYST Grace Livingston Hill	2705 ●	$1.25
☐	LOVE AND LAUGHTER Marjorie Holmes	2714 ●	$1.50
☐	MINE EYES HAVE SEEN THE GLORY Anita Bryant	2833 ●	$1.50
☐	THE WOMAN AT THE WELL Dale Evans Rogers	2866 ●	$1.50
☐	THE GREATEST SALESMAN IN THE WORLD Og Mandino	2930 ●	$1.75
☐	I'VE GOT TO TALK TO SOMEBODY, GOD Marjorie Holmes	2936 ●	$1.75
☐	HOW TO TALK TO GOD WHEN YOU AREN'T FEELING RELIGIOUS Charles Smith	7712 ●	$1.25
☐	THEY CALL ME COACH John Wooden	8146 ●	$1.50
☐	WHO AM I GOD? Marjorie Holmes	10210 ●	$1.75
☐	THE TASTE OF NEW WINE Keith Miller	10509 ●	$1.75
☐	TWO FROM GALILEE Marjorie Holmes	10756 ●	$1.75
☐	LIGHTHOUSE Eugenia Price	11180 ●	$1.75
☐	NEW MOON RISING Eugenia Price	11189 ●	$1.75
☐	THE LATE GREAT PLANET EARTH Hal Lindsey	11291 ●	$1.95

Buy them at your local bookstore or use this handy coupon for ordering:

INTIMATE REFLECTIONS

Thoughts, ideas, and perceptions of life as it is.

LOOKING IN

Books that explore Eastern and Western spirituality and examine man's concepts of God and the universe.

☐	THE GOSPEL ACCORDING TO PEANUTS Robert L. Short	2070 ●	$1.25
☐	"WITH GOD ALL THINGS ARE POSSIBLE!" Life Study Fellowship	2861 ●	$1.75
☐	THE GREATEST SALESMAN IN THE WORLD Og Mandino	2930 ●	$1.75
☐	MYTHS TO LIVE BY Joseph Campbell	7596 ●	$1.95
☐	GOD, MAN, AND ARCHIE BUNKER Spencer Marsh	7913 ●	$1.50
☐	THE BIBLE AS HISTORY: A CONFIRMATION OF THE BOOK OF BOOKS Werner Keller	10176 ●	$2.50
☐	THE PASSOVER PLOT Dr. Hugh J. Schonfield	10841 ●	$1.95
☐	I CHING: BOOK OF CHANGES Ch'u Chai, ed. with Windberg Chai	10989 ●	$1.95
☐	PSYCHOANALYSIS AND RELIGION Erich Fromm	11192 ●	$1.75
☐	MIRRORS OF THE SOUL Kahlil Gibran	11301 ●	$1.50

Buy them at your local bookstore or use this handy coupon for ordering:

Bantam Book Catalog

Here's your up-to-the-minute listing of every book currently available from Bantam.

This easy-to-use catalog is divided into categories and contains over 1400 titles by your favorite authors.

So don't delay—take advantage of this special opportunity to increase your reading pleasure.

Just send us your name and address and 25¢ (to help defray postage and handling costs).

BANTAM BOOKS, INC.
Dept. FC, 414 East Golf Road, Des Plaines, Ill. 60016

Mr./Mrs./Miss_____
(please print)

Address_____

City_____State_____Zip_____

Do you know someone who enjoys books? Just give us their names and addresses and we'll send them a catalog too!

Mr./Mrs./Miss_____

Address_____

City_____State_____Zip_____

Mr./Mrs./Miss_____

Address_____

City_____State_____Zip_____

FC—6/77